Quick-to-Stitch
HOLIDAY
PLASTIC CANVAS!

Edited by Laura Scott

HOUSE of
WHITE
BIRCHES

PUBLISHERS
SINCE 1947

Editor: Laura Scott
Associate Editor: June Sprunger
Copy Editor: Mary Nowak
Publications Coordinator: Tanya Turner
Technical Artists: Pam Gregory, Leslie Brandt, Allison Rothe, Jessica Rothe

Photography: Tammy Christian, Jeff Chilcote, Jennifer Fourman
Photography Stylist: Arlou Wittwer
Photography Assistant: Linda Quinlan

Production Coordinator: Brenda Gallmeyer
Book Design: Dan Kraner
Cover Design: Vicki Macy
Production Artist: Ronda Bechinski
Production Assistants: Shirley Blalock, Dana Brotherton, Carol Dailey
Traffic Coordinator: Sandra Beres

Publishers: Carl H. Muselman, Arthur K. Muselman
Chief Executive Officer: John Robinson
Marketing Director: Scott Moss
Product Development Director: Vivian Rothe
Publishing Services Manager: Brenda R. Wendling

Printed in the United States of America
First Printing: 2000
Library of Congress Number: 99-73198
ISBN: 1-882138-52-X

Every effort has been made to ensure the accuracy and completeness of the instructions
in this book. However, we cannot be responsible for human error or for the results when using
materials other than those specified in the instructions, or for variations in individual work.

HOLIDAY MAGIC
Is at Your Fingertips!

We know you'll enjoy crafting and sharing each of these merry projects with friends and family!

Dear Needlecrafters,

If there is one group of people who love holidays, it's needle-crafters! Crafters, and plastic canvas crafters in particular, just love creating festive projects for celebrating throughout the year.

Since all of us are busy, sometimes we struggle just to find the time to create all the projects we want for decorating the home, giving as gifts to family and friends, and selling at craft bazaars. This all-new collection of more than 100 festive holiday projects will make stitching easier and faster. Not only will you find bright, colorful and festive projects for celebrating every holiday from New Year's through Christmas, but you'll be able to make these projects in just a few hours.

In times past, most people considered Christmas to be the only major gift-giving and decorating occasion of the year. In recent years, however, as people everywhere have started to focus on the secondary holidays, our plastic canvas hobby has become a more important part in our celebrations. Nowadays, it's not uncommon to see coworkers giving one another hand-stitched Valentine's gifts, whimsical sprigs of green dressing up our St. Patrick's Day outfits, colorful Easter trees, patriotic accents, and cheery Halloween and Thanksgiving decorations indoors and out, in addition to oodles of Christmas accents and gifts galore!

Our goal is that you find this collection of projects, from whimsical and heartwarming to elegant and enchanting, a delight to stitch and share with your friends and family throughout the year.

Warm regards,

Laura Scott

Editor
Quick-to-Stitch Holiday Plastic Canvas

TABLE OF
Contents

New Year's Day

Valentine's Day

St. Patrick's Day

Easter

Mother's Day

Father's Day

Contents   Contents   Contents   Contents   Contents   Contents   Contents

TABLE OF
Contents

Thanksgiving

Fourth of July

Christmas

Halloween

Hanukkah

Contents   Contents   Contents   Contents   Contents   Contents   Contents

TIMES SQUARE
Party Hat

Design by Celia Lange Designs

Delight your family and friends with this fun and vibrant table centerpiece featuring New York City's Times Square.

Skill Level: Intermediate

Finished Size

Approximately 17" W x 21" H x 16" D

Materials

- 9" plastic canvas radial circle by Darice
- 2 (6") plastic canvas radial circles by Darice
- 1 sheet 7-count plastic canvas
- Coats & Clark Red Heart Classic worsted weight yarn Art. E267 as listed in color key
- Darice metallic cord as listed in color key
- Darice Bright Jewels metallic cord as listed in color key
- #16 tapestry needle
- 12" (⅛"-diameter) wooden dowel
- Silver acrylic paint
- Paintbrush
- Sheet black Fun Foam craft foam by Westrim Crafts
- Floral foam
- Sheet black tissue paper
- 18" (1"-wide) white and silver ribbon
- 2 (½") tinsel pompoms
- 10 (22mm) crystal clear star rhinestones #06308 by Darice
- 18" purple and royal blue mini star garland
- Shredded iridescent paper
- Large metallic spray picks with stars: 1 each in silver, magenta and purple
- Small metallic spray picks: 2 silver, 2 blue, 2 purple, 1 magenta, 1 aqua
- 2 (8") lengths 20-gauge florist wire
- Hot-glue gun

Cutting & Stitching

1. Cut hat crown, skylines, Empire State Buildings and year plaque pieces from plastic canvas according to graphs (page 8).

2. For hat top, cut center from one 6" radial circle, leaving only the four outer rows of holes. Do not cut the 9" radial circle, which is the hat brim, or the remaining 6" radial circle. The uncut 6" circle will remain unstitched.

3. Using black through step 7, Long Stitch around 9" circle from the outside row of holes over three bars to the fourth row of holes, working two stitches per hole as necessary in the fourth row of holes.

4. Moving toward the center, continue Long Stitching around circle from the fourth row of holes, over three bars to the seventh row of holes. Repeat pattern eight more times, until center holes are reached and entire circle is stitched. Overcast edge.

5. Long Stitch around the cut 6" hat top from the outside row of holes over three bars to the inside row of holes, working two stitches per hole as necessary in the inside row of holes. Overcast inside edge.

6. Work crown pieces following graph. Whipstitch wrong sides of crown pieces together along side edges, forming a tube.

7. Whipstitch top edge of crown to outside edge of hat top; Whipstitch bottom edge of crown to unstitched 6" circle.

8. Stitch remaining pieces following graphs. Overcast with adjacent colors.

Assembly

1. Paint dowel with silver paint, Allow to dry.

2. Using hat brim as a template, cut black craft foam to fit. Glue craft foam to wrong side of hat brim.

3. Trim block of floral foam to fit inside hat, so top of foam is about 1" from hat top. Form each length of wire into a "U" shape. Holding foam inside crown, insert wire ends through holes of unstitched 6" circle up into floral foam. Center and glue unstitched circle to right side of hat brim.

4. Crumble black tissue paper around floral foam, covering top of foam as well.

5. Using photo as a guide through step 9, wrap and glue 1"-wide white and silver ribbon around crown just above brim for hatband, trimming to fit.

6. Glue Empire State Buildings to opposite sides of crown over ribbon. Glue skylines to crown in front of Empire State Buildings.

7. Glue pompoms to tops of Empire State Buildings. Glue star rhinestones as desired to crown. Wrap purple and royal blue mini star garland around base of crown and glue in place.

8. Spread shredded iridescent paper inside top of hat to cover foam and tissue paper. Curl metallic picks as you would

curling ribbon. Bend star picks into swirls and curls. Insert picks through shredded paper and tissue into foam, arranging as desired.

9 Glue wrong sides of year plaques together over one end of painted dowel. Insert dowel into floral foam in center of arrangement.

COLOR KEY

Worsted Weight Yarn	Yards
■ Black #12	67
Metallic Cord	
▨ Silver #3411-02	10
■ Purple #3411-07	2
▨ Magenta #3411-08	4
□ White/silver #34021-112	31

Color numbers given are for Red Heart Classic worsted weight yarn Art. E267 and Darice metallic cord and Bright Jewels metallic cord.

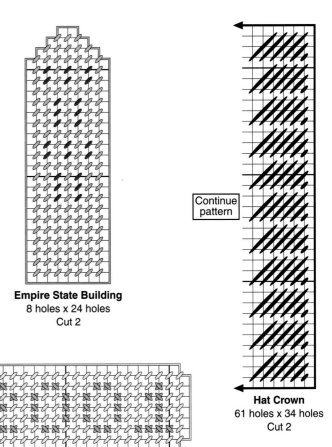

Empire State Building
8 holes x 24 holes
Cut 2

Continue pattern

Hat Crown
61 holes x 34 holes
Cut 2

Year Plaque
22 holes x 8 holes
Cut 2

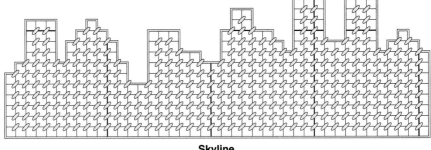

Skyline
41 holes x 13 holes
Cut 2

New Year's Day   New Year's Day   New Year's Day   New Year's Day   New Year's

NEW YEAR'S
Bear

Design by Angie Arickx

Clip your New Year's resolution to this charming teddy bear refrigerator magnet.

Skill Level: Beginner

Finished Size

4⅝" W x 6¾" H

Materials

- ½ sheet 7-count plastic canvas
- Uniek Needloft plastic canvas yarn as listed in color key
- DMC #3 pearl cotton as listed in color key
- #16 tapestry needle
- #22 tapestry needle
- 3 (1") pieces magnetic strip
- Hot-glue gun

Instructions

1. Cut plastic canvas according to graph.

2. With #16 tapestry needle, stitch piece following graph. Work uncoded area on head and hands with maple Continental Stitches; work uncoded background on banner with white Continental Stitches.

3. With plum pearl cotton and #22 tapestry needle, Backstitch and Straight Stitch letters on banner when background stitching is completed. Overcast following graph.

4. Glue one magnetic strip to backside of head and one to backside of banner on each end.

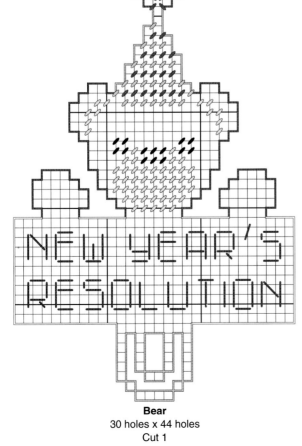

Bear
30 holes x 44 holes
Cut 1

COLOR KEY	
Plastic Canvas Yarn	**Yards**
■ Black #00	1
□ Beige #40	2
▨ Bright blue #60	3
▧ Bright pink #62	1
Uncoded areas on head and hands are maple #13 Continental Stitches	4
Uncoded area on banner is white #41 Continental Stitches	7
⁄ Maple #13 Overcasting	
⁄ White #41 Overcasting	
#3 Pearl Cotton	
⁄ Plum #718 Backstitch	
Color numbers given are for Uniek Needloft plastic canvas yarn and DMC #3 pearl cotton.	

New Year's Day   New Year's Day   New Year's Day   New Year's Day   New Year's Day

FESTIVE
Banner & Coaster

Designs by Angie Arickx

**Hang this colorful banner to get in the spirit of celebrating a new year.
The colorful coasters are perfect for New Year's Day football parties.**

Skill Level: Beginner

Finished Size

Banner: 18" W x 1½" H

Coaster: 3⅜" square

Materials

- ½ sheet 7-count plastic canvas
- Uniek Needloft plastic canvas yarn as listed in color key
- ⅛"-wide Plastic Canvas 7 Metallic Needlepoint Yarn by Rainbow Gallery as listed in color key
- #16 tapestry needle

Instructions

1. Cut one coaster, four stars and one of each word banner from plastic canvas according to graphs.

2. Stitch pieces following graphs, working uncoded areas with black Continental Stitches. Overcast coaster and banners with black; Overcast stars with silver.

3. Using photo as a guide, with silver, tack stars to banner tabs where indicated on graphs with blue dots, placing banners in sequence so message reads "HAPPY NEW YEAR."

4. Cut two 6" lengths of silver metallic needlepoint yarn. Thread ends from front to back at remaining blue dots on stars at each end of assembled banner. Tie ends in a knot.

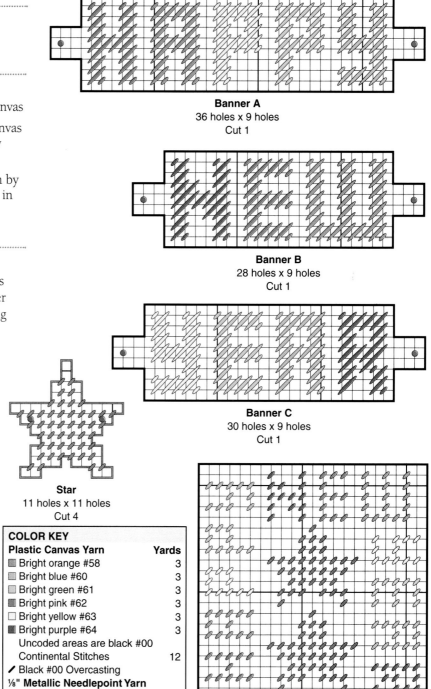

Banner A
36 holes x 9 holes
Cut 1

Banner B
28 holes x 9 holes
Cut 1

Banner C
30 holes x 9 holes
Cut 1

Star
11 holes x 11 holes
Cut 4

Coaster
22 holes x 22 holes
Cut 1

COLOR KEY

Plastic Canvas Yarn	Yards
Bright orange #58	3
Bright blue #60	3
Bright green #61	3
Bright pink #62	3
Bright yellow #63	3
Bright purple #64	3
Uncoded areas are black #00 Continental Stitches	12
Black #00 Overcasting	

⅛" Metallic Needlepoint Yarn

Silver #PC2	

Color numbers given are for Uniek Needloft plastic canvas yarn and Rainbow Gallery Plastic 7 Metallic Needlepoint Yarn.

w Year's Day   New Year's Day   New Year's Day   New Year's Day   New Year's Day

TOAST THE NEW YEAR
Napkin Holder

Design by Judy Collishaw

Create this unique napkin holder to add an extra-festive touch to your New Year's Eve party!

Skill Level: Intermediate

Finished Size

5" W x 5" H

Materials

- ⅓ sheet white 7-count plastic canvas
- Small amount red 7-count plastic canvas
- Uniek Needloft metallic craft cord as listed in color key
- Worsted weight yarn as listed in color key
- #16 tapestry needle
- Low-temperature glue gun

Instructions

1. Cut four goblets and two braces from white plastic canvas; cut one bow and two wine pieces from red plastic canvas according to graphs. Cut one 13-hole x 6-hole piece from white plastic canvas for the base.

2. Stitch and Overcast bow following graph. Do not stitch remaining pieces.

3. Overcast foot and stem of each goblet with white iridescent metallic cord. Whipstitch bottom edge of each brace to one long edge of base with white yarn.

4. Using photo as a guide, crisscross two goblets and Cross Stitch together where indicated on graph with white iridescent metallic cord. Repeat with remaining two goblets.

5. Place joined goblets together with wrong sides facing. Whipstitch sides of goblet bowls together with white iridescent metallic cord. Do not Overcast top edges of goblets.

6. Using white yarn, attach goblet feet to braces where indicated on graphs with blue dots.

7. Glue bow to goblet stems over the joining Cross Stitch. Place wine inside goblet bowls, matching shape of wine to bowl. ✎

Bow
9 holes x 10 holes
Cut 1 from red

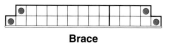

Brace
15 holes x 2 holes
Cut 2 from white
Do not stitch

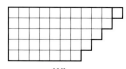

Wine
11 holes x 5 holes
Cut 2 from red
Do not stitch

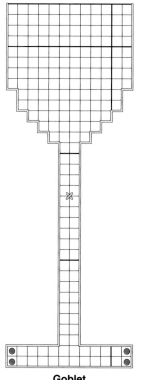

Goblet
12 holes x 34 holes
Cut 4 from white
Do not stitch

COLOR KEY	
Metallic Craft Cord	**Yards**
■ Red #03	2
⁄ White iridescent #33	
Overcasting and Whipstitching	10
Worsted Weight Yarn	
⁄ White Whipstitching	2
Color numbers given are Uniek Needloft craft cord.	

SWEET HEARTS
Pin

Design by Vicki Blizzard

Celebrate Valentine's Day with this delightful pin added to your February 14 outfit!

Skill Level: Beginner

Finished Size
Approximately 3¼" W x 6" H

Materials
- Small amount 7-count plastic canvas
- Uniek Needleloft plastic canvas yarn as listed in color key
- DMC #3 Pearl Cotton as listed in color key
- #16 tapestry needle
- 44" (¼"-wide) white satin ribbon
- 2 (8mm) wiggle eyes
- 1½" pin back
- Sewing needle and clear thread
- Hot-glue gun

Instructions

1. Cut plastic canvas according to graphs.

2. Stitch face, cheeks and heart dangles following graphs, stitching one dangle with lilac as graphed and one each with pink, baby yellow, baby green, sail blue and peach. Overcast stitched pieces with adjacent colors.

3. With light rose pearl cotton, work large Loop Stitch for mouth, tacking down loop where indicated on graph.

4. Separate a 12" length of white yarn into 1 ply to stitch and Overcast flower. Separate a 6" length of baby yellow yarn into 1 ply to work French Knot.

5. Cut ribbon into three 12" lengths and one 8" length. Fold each 12" length in half. Hold all three folded pieces together at folds. With sewing needle and clear thread, tack folds to center bottom back of face through all thicknesses of ribbon.

6. Using photo as a guide through step 8, glue one heart dangle to each ribbon at varying lengths; trim ribbon directly below each heart.

7. Tie remaining 8" ribbon into a small bow; trim ends. Glue bow to front bottom point of face.

8. Glue cheeks, wiggle eyes and flower to face.

9. Glue pin back to back of face.

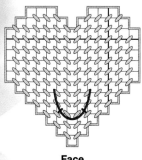

Face
13 holes x 13 holes
Cut 1

Cheek
3 holes x 3 holes
Cut 2

Flower
3 holes x 3 holes
Cut 1

Heart Dangle
5 holes x 5 holes
Cut 6
Stitch 1 as graphed and
1 each with pink, baby yellow,
baby green, sail blue and peach

COLOR KEY	
Plastic Canvas Yarn	**Yards**
■ Pink #07	2
▢ Baby pink #08	3
Baby yellow #21	1
Baby green #26	1
Sail blue #35	1
▢ White #41	½
▨ Lilac #45	1
Peach #47	1
○ Baby yellow #21 French Knot	
#3 Pearl Cotton	
∪ Light rose #3326 Loop Stitch	½
Color numbers given are for Uniek Needloft plastic canvas yarn and DMC #3 pearl cotton.	

VALENTINE
Picture Hoop

Design by Angie Arickx

Pretty hearts and a bow are glued around a small embroidery hoop to make a charming picture frame.

Skill Level: Beginner

Finished Size

4½" W x 5½" H

Materials

- Small amount 7-count plastic canvas
- 4½" plastic canvas radial circle by Darice
- Uniek Needloft plastic canvas yarn as listed in color key
- #16 tapestry needle
- 4" wooden embroidery hoop
- Photo or valentine card to fit hoop
- Heavy book or weight
- Craft glue

Instructions

1. Cut one hearts circle from 4½" radial circle; cut one bow from 7-count plastic canvas according to graphs.

2. Stitch and Overcast pieces following graphs.

3. Using photo as a guide, with watermelon, attach bow to screw shank of hoop. If desired, secure with a small amount of glue. Allow to dry.

4. Glue hearts circle to front of hoop, press with heavy book or weight and allow to dry.

5. Cut photo or valentine card in a circle to fit hoop, then glue to back of hoop.

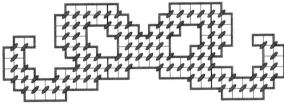

Bow
27 holes x 9 holes
Cut 1

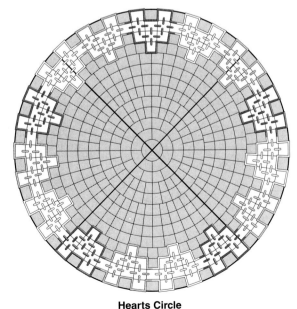

Hearts Circle
Cut 1
Cut away gray areas

COLOR KEY	
Plastic Canvas Yarn	**Yards**
■ Watermelon #55	7
⟋ Pink #07 Backstitch and Overcasting	3
⟋ White #41 Backstitch and Overcasting	3
⟍ Watermelon #55 Backstitch and Overcasting	
Color numbers given are for Uniek Needloft plastic canvas yarn.	

lentine's Day   Valentine's Day   Valentine's Day   Valentine's Day   Valentine's Day

HEARTS 'N' STRIPES
Mug & Coaster Set

Designs by Angie Arickx

Stitch this two-piece set for a close friend or co-worker as an expression of your affection.

Skill Level: Beginner

Finished Size

Mug Insert: Fits in a 3¼"-diameter acrylic mug with insert.

Coaster: 3⅝" W x 3½" H

Materials

- ½ sheet Darice Super Soft 7-count plastic canvas
- Uniek Needloft plastic canvas yarn as listed in color key
- Coats & Clark Red Heart Classic worsted weight yarn Art. E267 as listed in color key
- #16 tapestry needle
- White-rimmed plastic mug with insert area

Instructions

1. Cut plastic canvas according to graphs.

2. Stitch pieces following graphs. With pink, Overcast coaster; Whipstitch short edges of mug insert together, then Overcast top and bottom edges.

3. Place insert inside mug, aligning seam with handle.

COLOR KEY

Plastic Canvas Yarn	Yards
☐ Pink #07	12
■ Watermelon #55	10
Worsted Weight Yarn	
☐ White #1	12

Color numbers given are for Uniek Needloft plastic canvas yarn and Red Heart Clasic worsted weight yarn Art. E267.

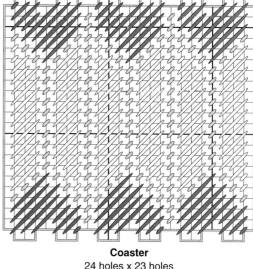

Coaster
24 holes x 23 holes
Cut 1

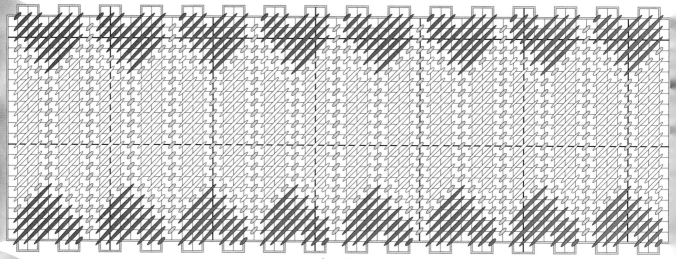

Insert
64 holes x 23 holes
Cut 1

Valentine's Day   Valentine's Day   Valentine's Day   Valentine's Day   Valentine's D

CONVERSATION
Hearts Trio

Designs by Ronda Bryce

Accented with dainty flowers and edged with lace, each of these three projects is a Valentine's gift that can be displayed and enjoyed throughout the year.

Skill Level: Beginner

Finished Size

7¼" in diameter including lace trim

Materials

- 3 (6") plastic canvas radial circles by Uniek
- 1 sheet 7-count plastic canvas
- Uniek Needloft plastic canvas yarn as listed in color key
- #16 tapestry needle
- 2¼ yards (1"-wide) white lace trim
- 27" (¼"-wide) white satin ribbon
- Sewing needle
- White sewing thread and thread to match frame yarns

Instructions

1. Cut away shaded gray area from radial circles for frames; cut message pieces from plastic canvas according to graphs (pages 19 and 20).

2. Stitch messages following graphs, working Backstitches and French Knots when background stitching is completed.

3. Stitch "Be Mine" frame with pink; Overcast with lavender. Stitch "Hug Me" frame with lemon; Overcast with pink. Stitch "Luv Ya" frame with mermaid; Overcast with lavender.

4. Using sewing needle and matching thread, center messages in frame openings and stitch in place.

5. Cut lace trim into three 27" lengths. Stitch one length to backside of each circle around outside edge, folding ends under and trimming to fit.

6. Cut ¼"-wide white satin ribbon into three 9" lengths. For each circle, thread ends of one ribbon length through a top center hole of message piece. Pull ends through until desired loop length is reached. Tie ends in a knot to secure. ❤

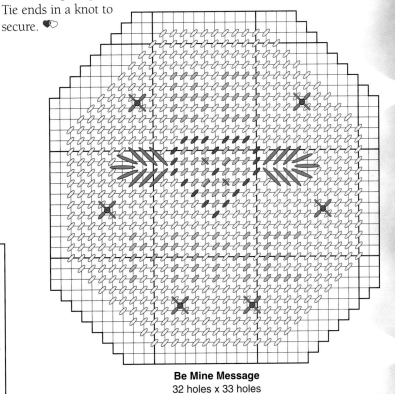

Frame
Cut 3
Cut away shaded gray area
Stitch Be Mine frame as graphed
Stitch Hug Me frame with lemon
Overcast with pink
Stitch Luv Ya frame with mermaid
Overcast with lavender

Be Mine Message
32 holes x 33 holes
Cut 1

COLOR KEY	
BE MINE	
Plastic Canvas Yarn	**Yards**
■ Lavender #05	6
▨ Pink #07	6
☐ Lemon #20	11
▨ Lilac #45	2
■ Mermaid #53	3
╱ Mermaid #53 Backstitch	
● Lavender #05 French Knot	
Color numbers given are for Uniek Needloft plastic canvas yarn.	

entine's Day   Valentine's Day   Valentine's Day   Valentine's Day   Valentine's Day

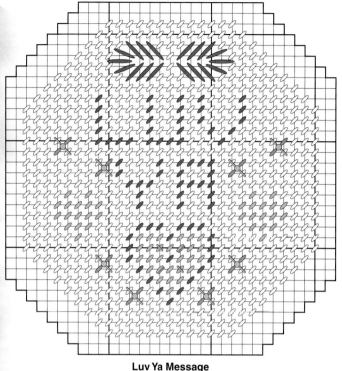

Luv Ya Message
32 holes x 33 holes
Cut 1

COLOR KEY
LUV YA

Plastic Canvas Yarn	Yards
■ Lavender #05	6
■ Pink #07	1
□ Baby pink #08	11
■ Lilac #45	2
■ Mermaid #53	6
╱ Mermaid #53 Backstitch	
● Lilac #45 French Knot	

Color numbers given are for Uniek Needloft plastic canvas yarn.

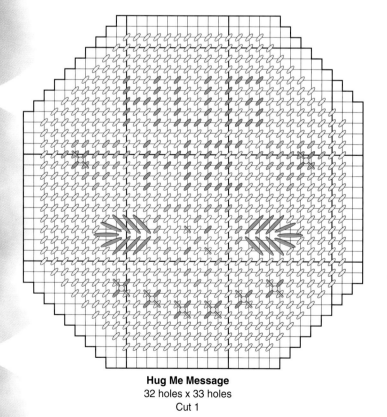

Hug Me Message
32 holes x 33 holes
Cut 1

COLOR KEY
HUG ME

Plastic Canvas Yarn	Yards
■ Pink #07	6
□ Baby pink #08	1
□ Lemon #20	7
□ Baby blue #36	11
■ Mermaid #53	3
╱ Mermaid #53 Backstitch	
○ Lemon #20 French Knot	

Color numbers given are for Uniek Needloft plastic canvas yarn.

Valentine's Day   Valentine's Day   Valentine's Day   Valentine's Day   Valentine's 1

TEDDY BEAR
Valentine

Design by Angie Arickx

*Give someone you love this sweet gift as a special Valentine.
It's just the right size for a bedside table or desk.*

Skill Level: Beginner

Finished Size

1¾" W x 2¾" H x 1¼" D

Materials

- ¼ sheet 7-count plastic canvas
- Uniek Needloft plastic canvas yarn as listed in color key
- #16 tapestry needle
- 1" brown flocked bear
- Hot-glue gun

Instructions

1. Cut plastic canvas according to graphs.

2. Stitch pieces following graphs. Do not stitch violet bow on chair back at this time. Legs will remain unstitched.

3. Using beige through step 4, Whipstitch back edge of chair seat to chair back where indicated on graph with a blue line.

4. Whipstitch remaining edges of chair seat to chair legs, then Whipstitch legs together. Overcast all remaining edges.

5. Work violet bow on chair back. Glue bear to chair seat. ❦

Back Edge

Seat
7 holes x 7 holes
Cut 1

COLOR KEY

Plastic Canvas Yarn	Yards
■ Christmas red #02	3
☐ Beige #40	4
╱ Violet #04 Backstitch and Straight Stitch	1

Color numbers given are for Uniek Needloft plastic canvas yarn.

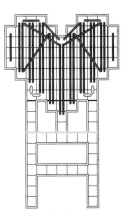

Back
11 holes x 18 holes
Cut 1

Cut out

Legs
7 holes x 7 holes
Cut 3
Do not stitch

VICTORIAN HEART
Potpourri Holder

Design by Ronda Bryce

This lovely project is just the right shape and size for holding a packet of potpourri.

Skill Level: Beginner

Finished Size

8" W x 6¾" H x 1" D including lace trim

Materials

- 2 (6") plastic canvas hearts by Uniek
- Small amount 7-count plastic canvas
- Spinrite plastic canvas yarn as listed in color key
- #16 tapestry needle
- 2 (1½") white ribbon petal roses with pearl centers #10-2709 by C.M. Offray & Son
- 18" (1"-wide) white lace trim
- 46 (4mm) white pearl beads
- 12" (¼"-wide) white satin ribbon
- Sewing needle and white thread

Instructions

1. Cut holder sides from plastic canvas according to graphs.

2. Stitch sides and holder front following graphs, working uncoded area on holder front with crimson Continental Stitches. Do not stitch holder back. With wine, Overcast rounded parts of both holder front and back from dot to dot.

3. Using sewing needle and white thread through step 4, attach pearl beads to front where indicated on graph.

4. Tack flowers to front as in photo. Sew lace trim to backside of front along rounded edges.

5. Using wine yarn and taking two stitches per hole throughout, Whipstitch long straight edges of sides to straight edges of front and back. Whipstitch adjoining edges of sides together. Overcast remaining edges.

6. For hanger, thread ends of ¼"-wide white satin ribbon through holes indicated on holder back. Tie ends in a knot.

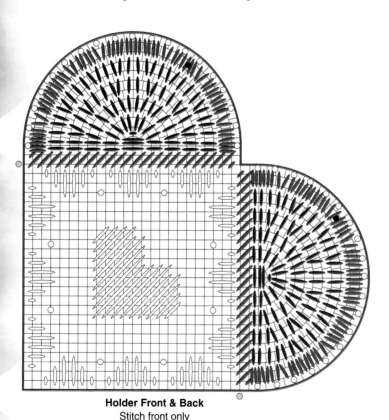

Holder Front & Back
Stitch front only

Holder Side
5 holes x 24 holes
Cut 2

COLOR KEY

Plastic Canvas Yarn	Yards
☐ White #0001	4
■ Wine #0011	12
■ Crimson #0032	13
○ Attach pearl beads	
● Attach white satin ribbon	

Color numbers given are for Spinrite plastic canvas yarn.

LOVE
Notes

Designs by Alida Macor

Stitch one of these keepsake cards for someone you love.
Your hand-stitched gift will surely be treasured for years to come.

Skill Level: Beginner

Finished Size

Card: 5½" W x 3¾" H

Stitched Message: 4¼" W x 3" H

Materials

Each Card

- ¼ sheet 10-count plastic canvas
- DMC #3 pearl cotton as listed in color key
- #22 tapestry needle

- Tri-fold needlework card with 2½" x 3½" heart opening from Yarn Tree Designs Inc.
- Craft glue or glue stick

Bee Mine

- 6-strand embroidery floss as listed in color key

Instructions

1. Cut plastic canvas according to graphs.

2. Stitch pieces with #3 pearl cotton following graphs. On Bee Mine card, work Backstitches for antennae and French Knot for flower center with 3 strands black embroidery floss. Using 1 strand black embroidery floss, work Backstitches to outline bee. Overcast following graphs.

3. For each stitched heart, center and glue right side of heart behind heart opening on one card. Allow to dry. Glue entire backside of heart to tri-fold flap adjacent to bottom of heart.

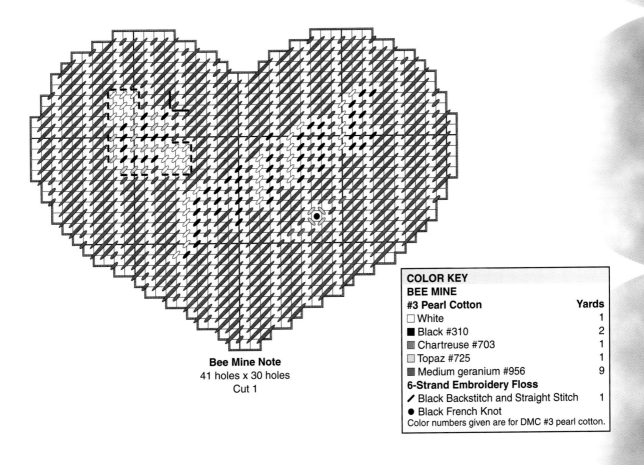

Bee Mine Note
41 holes x 30 holes
Cut 1

COLOR KEY
BEE MINE

#3 Pearl Cotton	Yards
☐ White	1
■ Black #310	2
▨ Chartreuse #703	1
☐ Topaz #725	1
▨ Medium geranium #956	9

6-Strand Embroidery Floss

✐ Black Backstitch and Straight Stitch	1
● Black French Knot	

Color numbers given are for DMC #3 pearl cotton.

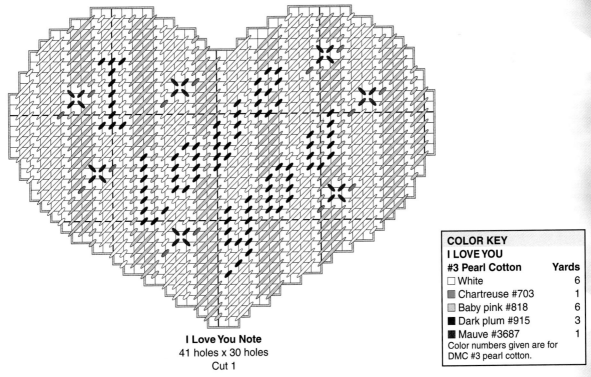

I Love You Note
41 holes x 30 holes
Cut 1

COLOR KEY
I LOVE YOU

#3 Pearl Cotton	Yards
☐ White	6
▨ Chartreuse #703	1
☐ Baby pink #818	6
■ Dark plum #915	3
▨ Mauve #3687	1

Color numbers given are for DMC #3 pearl cotton.

SWEETHEARTS
Photo Frame

Design by Mary T. Cosgrove

Always keep your loved ones in view with this Valentine's Day triple photo frame.

Skill Level: Beginner

Finished Size

6" W x 8" H

Materials

- ❥ 1 sheet Uniek Quick-Count 7-count plastic canvas
- ❥ Uniek Needloft plastic canvas yarn as listed in color key
- ❥ 4mm 100 percent pure silk embroidery ribbon by Bucilla as listed in color key
- ❥ DMC 6-strand rayon floss as listed in color key
- ❥ #16 tapestry needle

Instructions

1. Cut frame front from plastic canvas according to graphs. Cut one 39-hole x 53-hole piece for frame back. Frame back will remain unstitched.

2. Stitch front following graph, working uncoded area with white Continental Stitches. Overcast top edge and inside edges on front with Christmas red.

3. When background stitching and Overcasting are completed,

work silk ribbon embroidery. Using 6 strands rayon floss, Backstitch words at bottom of frame.

4. Attach photos behind openings as desired. Whipstitch frame back to frame front around side and bottom edges.

5. Hang as desired. ❥

COLOR KEY	
Plastic Canvas Yarn	**Yards**
■ Christmas red #02	7
▨ Pink #07	3
☐ White #41	22
Uncoded areas are white #41 Continental Stitches	
4mm Silk Embroidery Ribbon	
╱ Red #24-539 Backstitch	2
6-Strand Rayon Floss	
╱ Bright Christmas red #30666 Backstitch	2
● Bright Christmas red #30666 French Knot	
Color numbers given are for Uniek Needloft plastic canvas yarn, Bucilla 4mm 100 percent silk embroidery ribbon and DMC 6-strand rayon floss.	

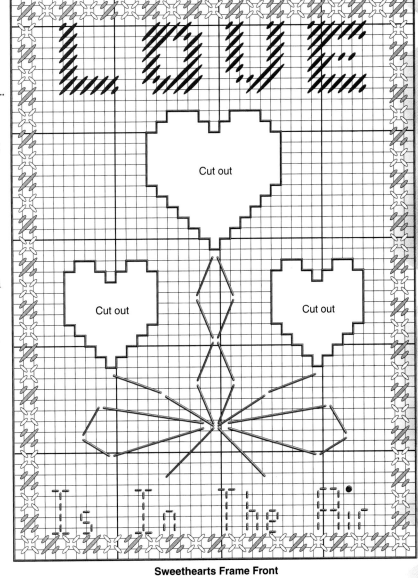

Sweethearts Frame Front
39 holes x 53 holes
Cut 1

LEPRECHAUN
Accents

Designs by Angie Arickx

*Invite a delightful leprechaun into your home by stitching
this magnet, pin and window ornament trio!*

Skill Level: Beginner

Finished Size

Magnet & Pin: 3" W x 3¾" H

Window Ornament:
Approximately 6⅛" W x 7" H

Materials

- ½ sheet Uniek Quick-Count 7-count plastic canvas
- Uniek Needloft plastic canvas yarn as listed in color key
- ⅛"-wide Plastic Canvas 7 Metallic Needlepoint Yarn by Rainbow Gallery as listed in color key
- DMC #3 pearl cotton as listed in color key
- #16 tapestry needle
- 1" magnetic strip
- 1" pin back
- Hot-glue gun

Instructions

1. Cut plastic canvas according to graphs.

2. Stitch pieces following graphs, working uncoded areas on leprechauns with baby pink Continental Stitches and uncoded area on banner with white Continental Stitches.

3. Work very dark mahogany Backstitches and Straight Stitches when background stitching is completed. Overcast following graphs.

4. Glue magnetic strip to backside of one leprechaun and pin back to backside of second leprechaun.

5. Using photo as a guide, for window ornament, cut a 12" length of Christmas green yarn for hanger. Thread length through hole indicated at top of remaining leprechaun.

6. Thread both ends of hanger yarn through stitches on center backside of banner, leaving ½"–¾" between banner and leprechaun and pulling remaining yarn through stitches on backside. Knot ends together at desired length.

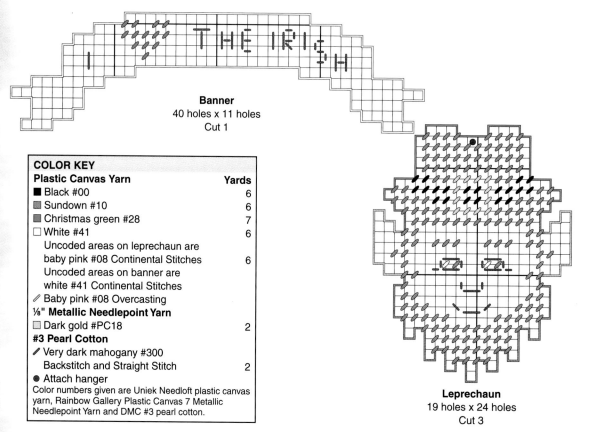

Banner
40 holes x 11 holes
Cut 1

COLOR KEY

Plastic Canvas Yarn	Yards
■ Black #00	6
▨ Sundown #10	6
▨ Christmas green #28	7
☐ White #41	6
Uncoded areas on leprechaun are baby pink #08 Continental Stitches	6
Uncoded areas on banner are white #41 Continental Stitches	
⁄ Baby pink #08 Overcasting	

⅛" Metallic Needlepoint Yarn

☐ Dark gold #PC18	2

#3 Pearl Cotton

⁄ Very dark mahogany #300 Backstitch and Straight Stitch	2
● Attach hanger	

Color numbers given are Uniek Needloft plastic canvas yarn, Rainbow Gallery Plastic Canvas 7 Metallic Needlepoint Yarn and DMC #3 pearl cotton.

Leprechaun
19 holes x 24 holes
Cut 3

St. Patrick's Day   St. Patrick's Day   St. Patrick's Day   St. Patrick's Day   St. Patrick's

POT O' GOLD
Favor

Design by Angie Arickx

Filled with gold foil-covered chocolates, this cheery favor will add a festive touch to St. Patrick's Day celebrations!

Skill Level: Beginner

Finished Size

4½" H x 3⅜" in diameter

Materials

- ½ sheet Uniek Quick-Count 7-count plastic canvas
- 3" Darice Crafty Circle
- Uniek Needloft plastic canvas yarn as listed in color key
- ⅛"-wide Plastic Canvas 7 Metallic Needlepoint Yarn by Rainbow Gallery as listed in color key
- #16 tapestry needle
- Hot-glue gun

Instructions

1. Cut plastic canvas according to graphs (pages 30 and 31).

2. Stitch pieces following graphs, overlapping three holes on pot side as indicated before stitching. Pot bottom, which is the 3" circle, will remain unstitched.

3. Overcast gold pieces and handle with dark gold. Overcast shamrocks with Christmas green. With black, Overcast top edge of pot; Whipstitch bottom edge to unstitched pot bottom.

4. Using photo as a guide through step 5, glue handle ends to opposite sides of pot. Glue gold pieces around top inside edge of pot.

5. Evenly space and glue six shamrocks around outside of pot. Tuck stem of remaining shamrock into a hole in handle.

Pot Shamrock
7 holes x 7 holes
Cut 7

Pot Gold Piece
5 holes x 5 holes
Cut 10

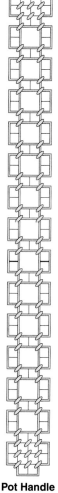

Pot Handle
4 holes x 46 holes
Cut 1

COLOR KEY	
Plastic Canvas Yarn	**Yards**
■ Black #00	11
▨ Christmas green #28	6
⅛" Metallic Needlepoint Yarn	
□ Dark gold #PC18	10
Color numbers given are for Uniek Needloft plastic canvas yarn and Rainbow Gallery Plastic Canvas 7 Metallic Needlepoint Yarn.	

SHAMROCK Pin

Design by Linda Wyszynski

Bring good luck to yourself this St. Patrick's Day by wearing this lucky shamrock pin!

Skill Level: Beginner

Finished Size
2¼" W x 2⅜" H

Materials
- Small amount 10-count plastic canvas
- DMC #3 pearl cotton as listed in color key
- #22 tapestry needle
- 1" pin back
- 1" (½"-wide) magnetic strip (optional)
- Hot-glue gun

Instructions
1. Cut plastic canvas according to graph.

2. Continental Stitch piece following graph. Overcast with very dark emerald green.

3. Glue pin back to backside of stitched piece, or if using as a magnet, glue magnet strip to backside.

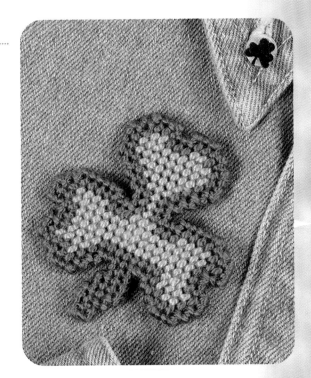

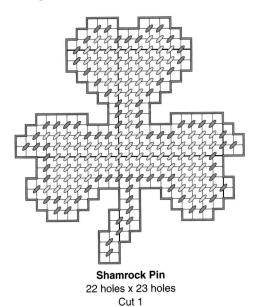

Shamrock Pin
22 holes x 23 holes
Cut 1

COLOR KEY	
#3 Pearl Cotton	**Yards**
■ Very dark emerald green #909	3
□ Medium Nile green #913	1½
Color numbers given are for DMC #3 pearl cotton.	

Pot O' Gold Favor

Continued from page 30

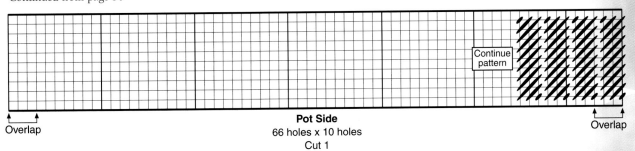

Pot Side
66 holes x 10 holes
Cut 1

Overlap

Continue pattern

Overlap

atrick's Day   St. Patrick's Day   St. Patrick's Day   St. Patrick's Day   St. Patrick's Day

SOW Lucky

Design by Vicki Blizzard

This Irish pig is ready to dance a Celtic jig into your heart and home!

Skill Level: Intermediate

Finished Size
Approximately 10½" W x 20" H

Materials

- 1 sheet Uniek Quick-Count 7-count plastic canvas
- 6" plastic canvas radial circle by Uniek
- 3 (3") plastic canvas radial circles by Darice
- Uniek Needleloft plastic canvas yarn as listed in color key
- Uniek Needleloft metallic craft cord as listed in color key
- #16 tapestry needle
- 1 yard 1"-wide green double-faced satin ribbon
- 3 green tinsel chenille stems
- 2 (12mm) round black cabochons from The Beadery
- Pencil
- Wire cutters
- Needle-nose pliers
- Hot-glue gun

Cutting & Stitching

1. From 3" radial circles, cut two cheek pieces and one snout front (pages 33 and 34).

2. Cut one bowler hat, one ear, two mouth pieces, one snout side, six shamrocks and one hanger from 7-count plastic canvas according to graphs (pages 33 and 34). Do not cut the 6" radial circle, which is the head.

3. Stitch pieces following graphs, reversing one mouth piece before stitching. Work

black Straight Stitches on snout front when background stitching is completed. Hanger will remain unstitched.

4. Using baby pink through step 5, roll snout side into a tube, overlapping two holes and placing left side on top of unstitched area on right side, then Whipstitch together with Continental Stitches. Whipstitch snout front to snout side. Overcast remaining edge of snout side.

5. Whipstitch mouth pieces together along short straight edges; Overcast remaining edges. Whipstitch dart edges of ear together. Overcast head.

6. Overcast cheeks and outside edges of ear with pink. Overcast hat with black.

Assembly

1. Using photo as a guide throughout assembly, glue cheeks

and snout to head, placing seam on snout at bottom. Glue mouth to head directly under snout, with straight edges facing out. Glue cabochons to head for eyes. Glue hat to head, slightly off center. Glue ear to head.

2. Tie ribbon in a bow with long streamers. Glue backside of sign to streamers on bow, approximately 3" from knot. Cut inverted "V" notches in streamer ends. Glue bow directly under mouth.

3. Cut each tinsel chenille stem in half with wire cutters. Wrap each piece around pencil. Slide coil loops off pencil. Thread one end of each coiled chenille stem through center bottom hole of one shamrock, using needle-nose pliers to pull end through; twist to secure. Thread opposite end of stems through hat and sign as desired.

4. Glue unstitched hanger to back of head at center top.

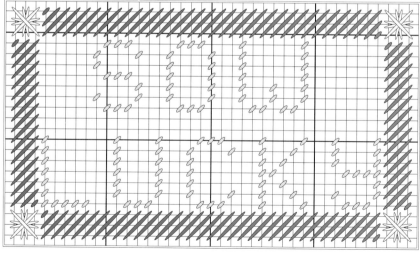

Sign
40 holes x 23 holes
Cut 1

St. Patrick's Day   St. Patrick's Day   St. Patrick's Day   St. Patrick's Day   St. Patrick's

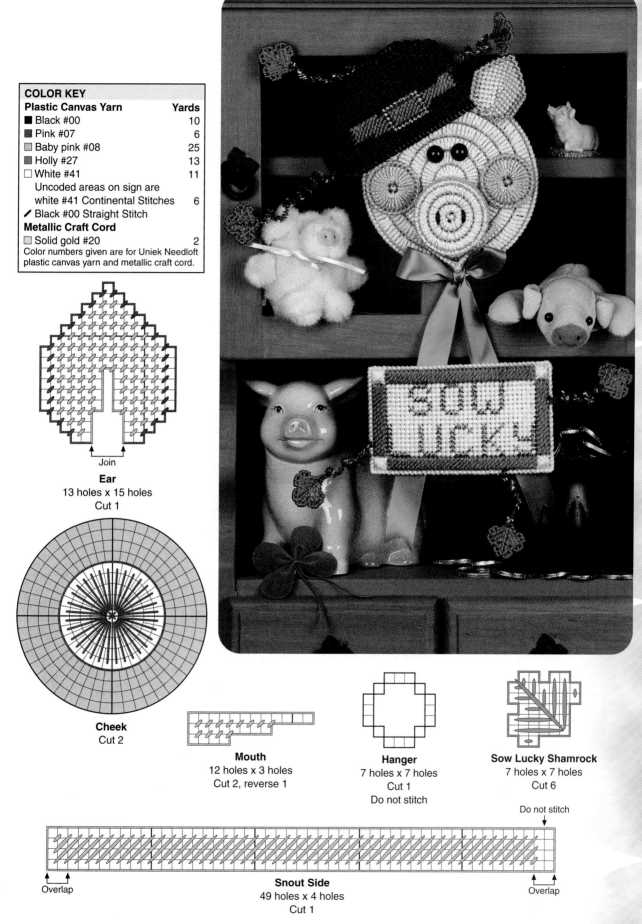

COLOR KEY

Plastic Canvas Yarn	Yards
■ Black #00	10
■ Pink #07	6
▨ Baby pink #08	25
▨ Holly #27	13
☐ White #41	11
Uncoded areas on sign are white #41 Continental Stitches	6
✎ Black #00 Straight Stitch	
Metallic Craft Cord	
☐ Solid gold #20	2

Color numbers given are for Uniek Needloft plastic canvas yarn and metallic craft cord.

Ear
13 holes x 15 holes
Cut 1

Join

Cheek
Cut 2

Mouth
12 holes x 3 holes
Cut 2, reverse 1

Hanger
7 holes x 7 holes
Cut 1
Do not stitch

Sow Lucky Shamrock
7 holes x 7 holes
Cut 6

Do not stitch

Snout Side
49 holes x 4 holes
Cut 1

Overlap

Overlap

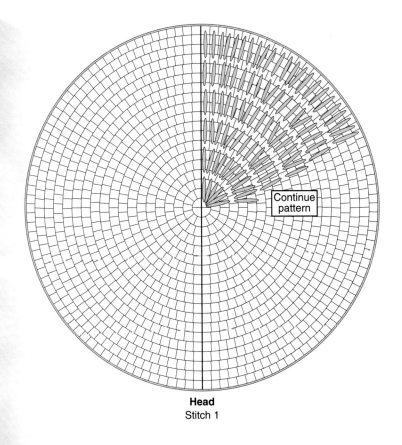

Head
Stitch 1

COLOR KEY	
Plastic Canvas Yarn	**Yards**
■ Black #00	10
■ Pink #07	6
■ Baby pink #08	25
■ Holly #27	13
□ White #41	11
Uncoded areas on sign are white #41 Continental Stitches	6
✦ Black #00 Straight Stitch	
Metallic Craft Cord	
□ Solid gold #20	2
Color numbers given are for Uniek Needloft plastic canvas yarn and metallic craft cord.	

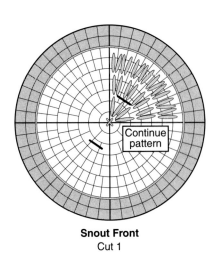

Snout Front
Cut 1

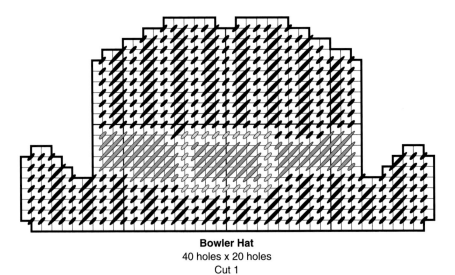

Bowler Hat
40 holes x 20 holes
Cut 1

SHAMROCK
Window Decoration

Design by Kathleen J. Fischer

Stick this glittering shamrock on a window in your home for a jolly splash of green! See photo on page 36.

Skill Level: Beginner

Finished Size
8⅛" W x 7¾" H

Materials
- 1 sheet 7-count plastic canvas
- Worsted weight yarn as listed in color key

- ⅛"-wide Plastic Canvas 7 Metallic Needlepoint Yarn by Rainbow Gallery as listed in color key
- #16 tapestry needle
- 1¾" suction cup

Instructions

1. Cut plastic canvas according to graphs (pages 35 and 37).

2. Stitch pieces following graphs. Overcast inside edges on back with green yarn.

3. Insert suction cup into cut-out area on back. Match edges and Whipstitch wrong sides of front and back together with green yarn.

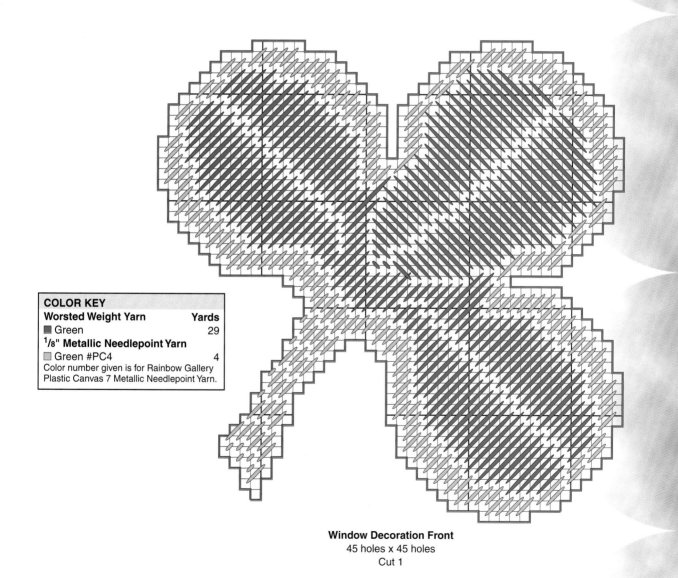

COLOR KEY	
Worsted Weight Yarn	**Yards**
■ Green	29
⅛" Metallic Needlepoint Yarn	
☐ Green #PC4	4
Color number given is for Rainbow Gallery Plastic Canvas 7 Metallic Needlepoint Yarn.	

Window Decoration Front
45 holes x 45 holes
Cut 1

rick's Day   St. Patrick's Day   St. Patrick's Day   St. Patrick's Day   St. Patrick's Day

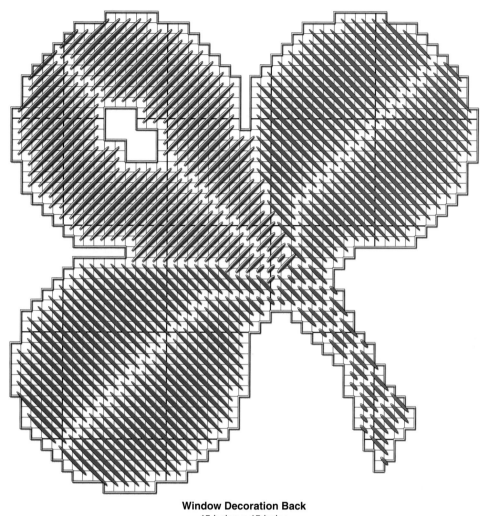

Window Decoration Back
45 holes x 45 holes
Cut 1

COLOR KEY	
Worsted Weight Yarn	**Yards**
■ Green	29
¹/₈" Metallic Needlepoint Yarn	
▨ Green #PC4	4
Color number given is for Rainbow Gallery Plastic Canvas 7 Metallic Needlepoint Yarn.	

BABY BUNNY
Basket

Design by Vicki Blizzard

Your child will fall in love with this cute bunny basket. With her fluffy tail and pink satin ribbon, she's just as sweet as can be!

Skill Level: Beginner

Finished Size
5¾" W x 7⅜" H x 5¾" D excluding bunny and flowers

Materials
- 2 sheets Uniek Quick-Count clear 7-count plastic canvas
- ½ sheet Uniek Quick-Count pastel blue 7-count plastic canvas
- Uniek Needloft plastic canvas yarn as listed in color key
- #16 tapestry needle
- 8mm round black cabochon from The Beadery
- 6 (½") light pink pompoms
- 6 (½") yellow pompoms
- 1" white pompom
- 15" 1"-wide light pink double-face satin ribbon

- Hot-glue gun

Instructions

1. Cut bunny pieces, flowers, basket sides and basket handle from clear plastic canvas according to graphs (pages 38 and 40). Cut one 37-hole x 37-hole piece from pastel blue plastic canvas for basket bottom.

2. Basket bottom will remain unstitched. Stitch remaining pieces following graphs, working six flowers with pink as graphed and six with straw.

3. Overcast flowers, legs and body with adjacent colors. Overcast bunny ear with tan. Using baby green throughout, Overcast handle and top edges of basket sides. Whipstitch sides together, then Whipstitch sides to bottom.

4. Glue one yellow pompom to center of each pink flower and one pink pompom to center of each straw flower.

5. Using photo as a guide through step 7, glue back and front legs to body. Glue ear to head. Glue cabochon to face for eye where indicated on graph. Glue white pompom to body for tail.

6. Glue bunny to one side of basket, making this the basket front. Glue handle ends to right sides of basket sides. Glue one pink flower to handle and one yellow flower to basket front beside bunny. Glue remaining flowers in clusters to basket sides and back.

7. Tie ribbon in a bow; trim ends. Glue bow to bunny's neck. ◉

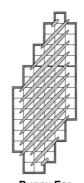

Bunny Ear
6 holes x 15 holes
Cut 1 from clear

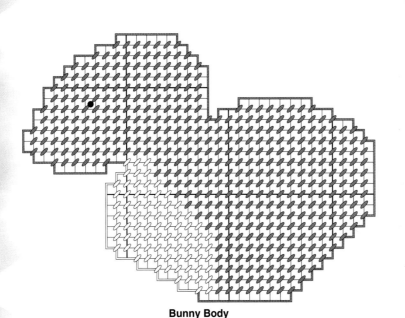

Bunny Body
34 holes x 25 holes
Cut 1 from clear

COLOR KEY	
Plastic Canvas Yarn	**Yards**
☐ Pink #07	9
■ Tan #18	14
☐ Straw #19	8
▨ Baby green #26	35
▨ Sail blue #35	27
☐ White #41	2
● Attach black cabochon	
Color numbers given are for Uniek Needloft plastic canvas yarn.	

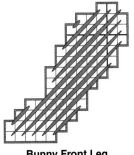

Bunny Front Leg
12 holes x 13 holes
Cut 1 from clear

COLOR KEY	
Plastic Canvas Yarn	**Yards**
☐ Pink #07	9
■ Tan #18	14
☐ Straw #19	8
☐ Baby green #26	35
☐ Sail blue #35	27
☐ White #41	2
● Attach black cabochon	

Color numbers given are for Uniek
Needloft plastic canvas yarn.

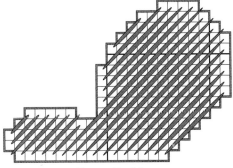

Bunny Back Leg
22 holes x 15 holes
Cut 1 from clear

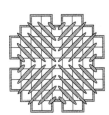

Flower
9 holes x 9 holes
Cut 12 from clear
Stitch 6 as graphed
Stitch 6 with straw

Continue
pattern

Baby Bunny Basket Handle
85 holes x 7 holes
Cut 1 from clear

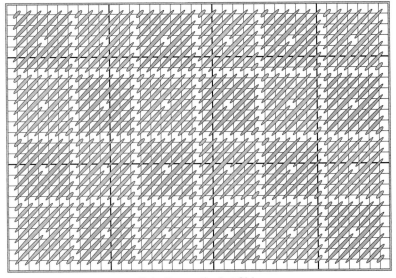

Baby Bunny Basket Side
37 holes x 25 holes
Cut 4 from clear

MINIATURE
Violet Basket

Design by Angie Arickx

Filled with jelly beans and chocolate eggs, this colorful spring cup makes a delightful party favor!

Skill Level: Beginner

Finished Size

5⅛" H x 3⅞" in diameter

Materials

- 1 sheet Uniek Quick-Count 7-count plastic canvas
- Uniek Needloft plastic canvas yarn as listed in color key
- #16 tapestry needle
- Hot-glue gun

Instructions

1. Cut plastic canvas according to graphs.

2. Following graphs, stitch basket sides and basket handle; stitch and Overcast violets, working French Knots last. Basket bottom will remain unstitched.

3. Overcast top edges of sides with fern. Using white throughout, Overcast handle. Whipstitch sides together, then Whipstitch sides to bottom.

4. Using red dots for placement, glue violets to basket sides. Using photo as a guide, glue handle ends inside basket.

COLOR KEY

Plastic Canvas Yarn	Yards
Fern #23	5
White #41	14
Bright purple #64	6
Straw #19 French Knot	2

Color numbers given are for Uniek Needloft plastic canvas yarn.

Violet
5 holes x 5 holes
Cut 8

Miniature Basket Side
11 holes x 14 holes
Cut 8

Miniature Basket Handle
41 holes x 41 holes
Cut 1

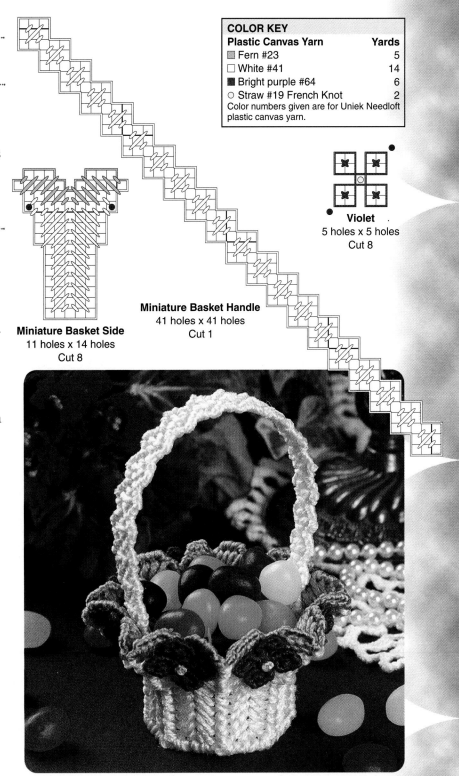

Miniature Basket Bottom
13 holes x 13 holes
Cut 1
Do not stitch

EASTER EGG
Animals

Designs by Janelle Giese

*These bunny and duck Easter egg cups are just the right size
for holding a colored egg or other candies and treats!*

Skill Level: Intermediate

Finished Size
Bunny: 2¾" W x 3¼" H x 4" D
Duck: 2¾" W x 2⅝" H x 3¾" D

Materials
- ⅔ sheet 7-count plastic canvas
- Lion Chenille acrylic yarn Article #710 from Lion Brand Yarn Co. as listed in color key
- DMC #8 pearl cotton as listed in color key
- #16 tapestry needle
- Hot-glue gun

Project Note
When stitching egg cups, work with 18" lengths of chenille yarn.

Instructions

1. Cut plastic canvas according to graphs.

2. Stitch duck and bunny heads and duck tail following graphs. Using adjacent colors, Overcast all but bottom edges of each head and duck tail.

3. Stitch embroidery with black pearl cotton, working six stitches for each eye. For nose on bunny, use 2 strands natural yarn.

4 Stitch and Overcast feet on bases following graphs. Embroider toes with black pearl cotton.

5. Using white for bunny and yellow for duck, Whipstitch bottom edges of heads to corresponding bases where indicated on graph with blue line.

6. Stitch egg cup sides following graph, overlapping two holes before stitching and working one cup side with white for bunny and one cup side with yellow for

duck. Overcast top edges with adjacent colors.

7. Using white and placing overlapped area on bunny side behind head on base, Whipstitch side to unstitched area on base. *Note: There will be one unstitched bar between head and cup side on base.* Glue head to side.

8. Repeat step 7 for duck using yellow yarn, Whipstitching duck tail to side and base where indicated on graph.

9. For bunny tail, wrap one yard of white yarn around two fingers. Tie a separate strand of yarn around center, knotting tightly. Do not trim tails of tied strand. Cut loops and separate strands into a pompom. Thread tails of center tie through holes of egg cup on back of animal; knot to secure.

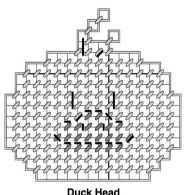

Duck Head
17 holes x 16 holes
Cut 1

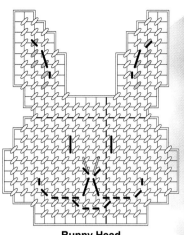

Bunny Head
17 holes x 20 holes
Cut 1

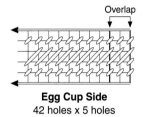

Overlap

Egg Cup Side
42 holes x 5 holes
Cut 2
Stitch 1 as graphed for bunny
Stitch 1 with yellow for duck

Attach duck tail

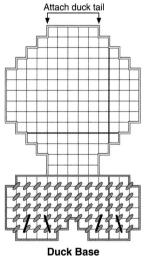

Duck Base
13 holes x 20 holes
Cut 1

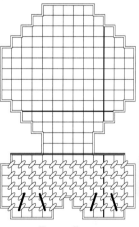

Bunny Base
13 holes x 20 holes
Cut 1

Duck Tail
5 holes x 5 holes
Cut 1

EASTER EGG
Door Decoration

Design by Joan Green

Display this colorful door decoration to celebrate the Easter season year after year!

Skill Level: Beginner

Finished Size

7¼" W x 13" H

Materials

- ⅔ sheet 7-count plastic canvas
- Spinrite Bernat Berella "4" worsted weight yarn as listed in color key
- Spinrite plastic canvas yarn as listed in color key
- #16 tapestry needle
- 1 yard 1½"-wide pink sheer wire-edge ribbon
- 5 white cotton chenille stems

Instructions

1. Cut plastic canvas according to graphs.

2. Stitch eggs following graphs. When background stitching is completed, work Backstitches and French Knots with 2 plies yarn.

3. Whipstitch top darts of each egg together with adjacent colors. Repeat with bottom darts. Overcast remaining edges of each egg following graphs.

4. Glue a chenille stem to back of each shaped egg, placing one end at bottom of each egg.

5. Using photo as a guide, arrange eggs for hanging. Cut off excess chenille stems on two top eggs. Twist all five ends tightly together.

6. Cut pink sheer ribbon in half. Place both lengths together and tie in a bow; trim tails as desired. Glue bow to top of chenille stems.

7. Lightly glue edges of eggs together along adjacent edges.

8. Hang as desired.

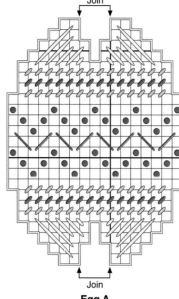

Egg A
17 holes x 23 holes
Cut 1

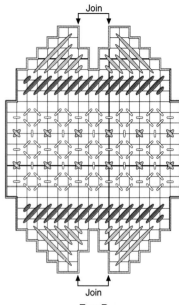

Egg B
17 holes x 23 holes
Cut 1

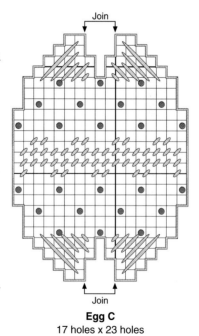

Egg C
17 holes x 23 holes
Cut 1

COLOR KEY

Worsted Weight Yarn	Yards
☐ Sunshine #8701	3
■ Arbutus #8922	3
☐ Baby yellow #8945	6
Uncoded areas on egg D are white #8941 Continental Stitches	6
Uncoded area on egg E is baby blue #8944 Continental Stitches	3
Uncoded area on egg A is baby yellow #8945 Continental Stitches	
Uncoded areas on egg C are baby green #8948 Continental Stitches	4
⁄ White #8941 Backstitch and Overcasting	
⁄ Baby green #8948 Overcasting	
⁄ Arbutus #8922 Backstitch	
○ Sunshine #8701 French Knot	
● Arbutus #8922 French Knot	
Plastic Canvas Yarn	
▨ Peach #0007	6
■ Lilac #0008	5
▨ Cherry blossom #0010	7
■ Robin #0016	6
Uncoded background on egg B is robin #0016 Continental Stitches	
● Lilac #0008 French Knot	

Color numbers given are for Spinrite Bernat Berella "4" worsted weight yarn and plastic canvas yarn.

Easter   Easter   Easter   Easter   Easter   Easter   Easter   Easter   Easter   Ea

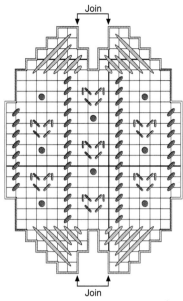

Egg D
17 holes x 23 holes
Cut 1

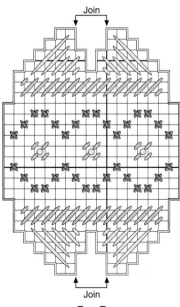

Egg E
17 holes x 23 holes
Cut 1

EASTER SUNDAY
Bread Basket

Design by Ronda Bryce

Treat your family to hot-cross buns served in this colorful and inspirational bread basket on Easter Sunday.

Skill Level: Beginner

Finished Size

8½" H x 9½" in diameter

Materials

- 6 sheets white 7-count plastic canvas
- Spinrite plastic canvas yarn as listed in color key
- #16 tapestry needle
- ½" ribbon roses: 1 peach, 1 yellow, 2 blue, 2 beige, 2 pink and 9 white
- 2 yards ⅝"-wide white wire-edge ribbon
- Bread cloth at least 16" square
- Sewing needle and white thread

Cutting & Stitching

1. Cut plastic canvas according to graphs (pages 47 and 48).

2. For each of the eight crosses and for basket handle, place two pieces together and stitch as one following graphs, stitching one cross with lemon, one with peach, two with seafoam, two with pale pink and two with sky. Basket bottom will remain unstitched.

3. For lemon, peach, seafoam and pale pink crosses, Overcast all outside edges except bottom edge with adjacent colors. Do not Overcast inside edges.

4. Using sky, Overcast long straight edges of handle and all outside edges except top and bottom edges of sky crosses.

Assembly

1. Use photo as a guide through-out assembly. Place two base pieces together, matching edges. Whipstitch bottom edges of crosses to base where indicated on base graph with adjacent cross colors.

2. Cut a 54" length of white ribbon. Beginning at center of one cross, bring ribbon from back to front through one center slit. Pull ribbon over unstitched area on front of cross and thread from front to back through second center slit.

3. Continue by weaving ribbon from back to front through crossbar slit, then from front to back through crossbar slit on adjacent cross.

4. Continue weaving ribbon through all crosses until starting point is reached. Trim ends and turn under, overlapping about ½". Sew ends together and to crossbar with sewing needle and white thread. With sky, Overcast remaining edges of base, working two stitches per hole.

5. Weave remaining 18" length of ribbon through slits on handle. Trim ends and turn under. With sewing needle and white thread, sew ends to backside of handle. With sky, Whipstitch handle ends to top edges of blue crosses.

6. With sewing needle and white thread, sew white ribbon roses to ribbon squares on handle. Matching ribbon rose colors with cross colors, sew remaining ribbon roses to center of crosses, placing beige roses with seafoam crosses.

7. Place bread cloth in basket.

COLOR KEY

Plastic Canvas Yarn	Yards
Pale pink #0003	10
Sky #0004	23
Lemon #0006	5
Peach #0006	5
Seafoam #0013	10
Pale pink #0003 Whipstitching	
Peach #0007 Whipstitching	
Seafoam #0013 Whipstitching	

Color numbers given are for Spinrite plastic canvas yarn.

Bread Basket Cross
25 holes x 34 holes
Cut 16
For each cross, place two together and stitch as one
Stitch one as graphed,
one with peach and
two each with seafoam,
pale pink and sky

er Easter Easter Easter Easter Easter Easter Easter Easter Easter

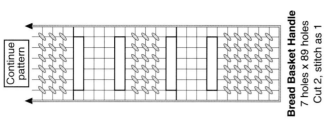

Bread Basket Handle
7 holes x 89 holes
Cut 2, stitch as 1

Continue pattern

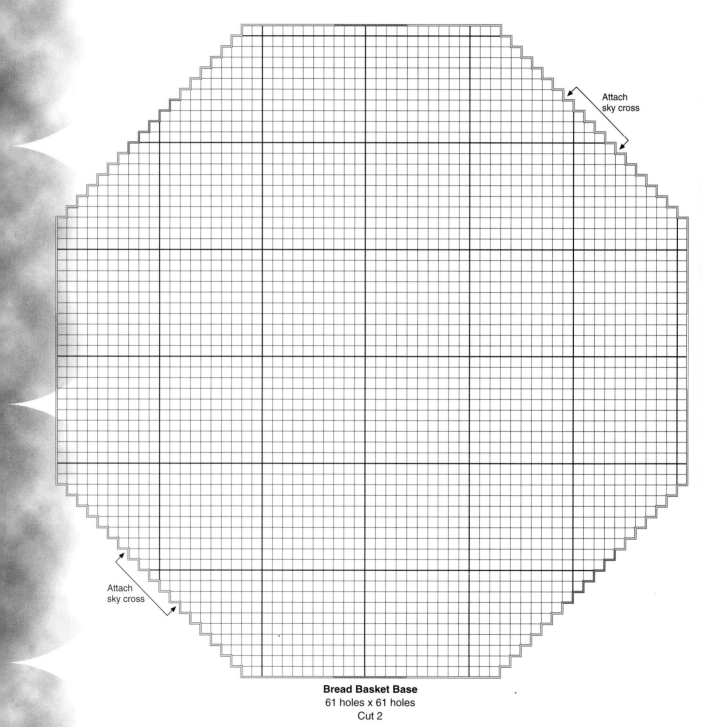

Attach sky cross

Attach sky cross

Bread Basket Base
61 holes x 61 holes
Cut 2

Easter   Easter   Easter   Easter   Easter   Easter   Easter   Easter   Easter   Ea

EASTER PEARLS
Ornaments

Designs by Vicki Blizzard

Hang these plastic canvas eggs on a branch painted white for a festive Easter decoration.

Skill Level: Beginner

Finished Size

Approximately 4½" W x 7" H including ribbon

Materials

- 1 sheet Uniek Quick-Count 7-count plastic canvas
- Uniek Needloft plastic canvas yarn as listed in color key
- #16 tapestry needle
- 508 (3.5mm) white pearl beads
- 4½ yards 1"-wide white double-face satin ribbon
- Sewing needle and white sewing thread
- Polyester fiberfill
- Hot-glue gun

Instructions

1. Cut plastic canvas according to graphs (pages 49 and 51).

2. Stitch pieces following graphs. With sewing needle and white sewing thread, attach pearls where indicated on graphs.

3. Using white throughout, Overcast top edges from arrow to arrow. For each egg, Whipstitch wrong sides of front and back together around sides and bottom, stuffing with fiberfill before Whipstitching is completed.

4. Cut ribbon into six 12" lengths and six 15" lengths. Place nozzle of glue gun in top opening of one egg and insert a glob of glue. Fold one 12" length of ribbon in half and insert cut ends into opening, pushing into glue. Press top opening together and hold until glue sets. Repeat for each egg.

5. Using photo as a guide, tie each 15" length of ribbon in a bow; trim a "V" notch in ends. Glue one bow to top of each egg.

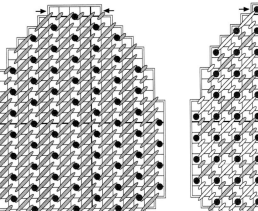

Egg A
17 holes x 21 holes
Cut 2

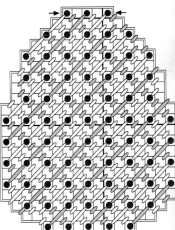

Egg B
17 holes x 21 holes
Cut 2

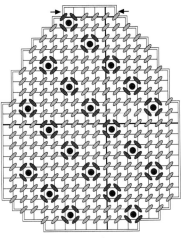

Egg C
17 holes x 21 holes
Cut 2

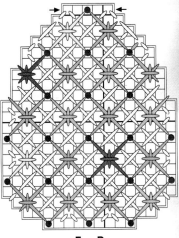

Egg D
17 holes x 21 holes
Cut 2

COLOR KEY	
Plastic Canvas Yarn	**Yards**
Pink #07	17
Baby yellow #21	10
Baby green #26	11
Sail blue #35	9
White #41	17
Lilac #45	5
Peach #47	7
● Attach pearl bead	
Color numbers given are for Uniek Needloft plastic canvas yarn.	

ster   *Easter*   *Easter*   *Easter*   *Easter*   *Easter*   *Easter*   *Easter*   *Easter*   *Easter*

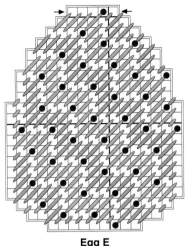

Egg E
17 holes x 21 holes
Cut 2

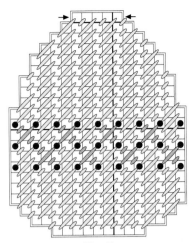

Egg F
17 holes x 21 holes
Cut 2

COLOR KEY

Plastic Canvas Yarn	Yards
▨ Pink #07	17
☐ Baby yellow #21	10
▨ Baby green #26	11
▨ Sail blue #35	9
☐ White #41	17
▧ Lilac #45	5
▨ Peach #47	7
● Attach pearl bead	

Color numbers given are for Uniek
Needloft plastic canvas yarn.

TULIP
Gift Bag

Design by Vicki Blizzard

**Delight Mom with two gifts in one by tucking
this year's Mother's Day gift inside this cheerful gift bag!**

Skill Level: Beginner

Finished Size

7" W x 6½" H x 2⅝" D

Materials

❋ 1 sheet Uniek Quick-Count clear 7-count plastic canvas

❋ ¼ sheet Uniek Quick-Count white 7-count plastic canvas

❋ Uniek Needloft plastic canvas yarn as listed in color key

❋ #16 tapestry needle

❋ Hot-glue gun

Instructions

1. Cut front, back, sides and leaves from clear plastic canvas according to graphs. Cut one 37-hole x 13-hole piece from white for bag bottom. Bag bottom will remain unstitched.

2. Stitch remaining pieces following graphs. Overcast leaves with holly. Using white throughout, Overcast top edges of front, back and sides. Whipstitch front and back to sides, then Whipstitch front, back and sides to unstitched bottom.

3. Using photo as a guide, glue leaves to stems on bag front and back.

4. For handle, cut a 2 yard length of holly yarn. Tie ends in a knot to form a circle. Loop circle over index fingers of both hands. Twist fingers in opposite directions, twisting yarn until it begins to loop back on itself. Place both loops on one index finger, folding yarn in half; allow halves to twist around each other.

5. Tie a knot in one end. Measure 10" from knot and tie another knot. Trim ends approximately ¼" from knots. Repeat for second handle.

6. Thread ends of a 9" length of holly yarn from outside to inside of bag at corner, three holes down on right side of bag front and bag side, forming a loop on the outside.

7. Slip one end of one handle through loop so knot is just below loop. Pull loop tight and tie ends in a knot on inside of

bag; trim ends. Repeat with other end of handle on left side of bag front.

8. Repeat steps 6 and 7 with remaining handle on bag back. ❋

COLOR KEY	
Plastic Canvas Yarn	**Yards**
■ Red #01	4
□ Straw #19	8
▨ Holly #27	26
□ White #41	90
▨ Watermelon #55	4
Color numbers given are for Uniek Needloft plastic canvas yarn.	

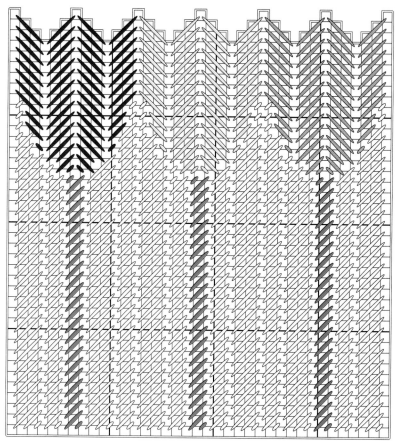

Bag Front & Back
37 holes x 40 holes
Cut 2 from clear

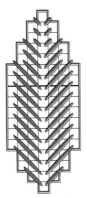

Tulip Leaf
7 holes x 17 holes
Cut 8 from clear

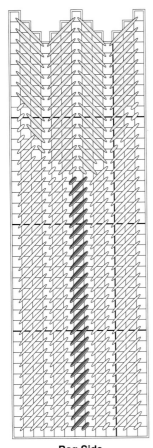

Bag Side
13 holes x 40 holes
Cut 2 from clear

Mother's Day   Mother's Day   Mother's Day   Mother's Day   Mother's Day

MOTHER'S TRIPLE
Photo Frame

Design by Joan Green

**Give your mother a special gift this Mother's Day by framing
three of her favorite photographs in this attractive frame.**

Skill Level: Beginner

Finished Size

16½" W x 7⅝" H

Materials

❁ 1 (12" x 18") sheet Darice Ultra Stiff 7-count plastic canvas

❁ Spinrite Bernat Berella "4" worsted weight yarn as listed in color key

❁ #16 tapestry needle

❁ 20" ⅛"-wide pink satin ribbon

❁ Lightweight white cardboard

❁ Hot-glue gun or thick white craft glue

Instructions

1. Cut three frames from plastic canvas according to graph.

2. For each frame, cut one lightweight cardboard slightly smaller all around than frame.

3. Stitch frames following graphs. When background stitching is completed, work light sea green Backstitches and rose and arbutus French Knots with 4 plies yarn. Work Backstitches around hearts with 2 plies arbutus.

4. Using dark denim throughout, Overcast inside edges. Whipstitch two frames together along one straight side edge. Repeat with third frame so that all three frames are stitched together in one long strip. Overcast all remaining edges.

5. Cut pink ribbon in half. Thread one length from back to front through holes indicated on first and second frames. Tie in a

bow; trim ends. Repeat with remaining ribbon threading through holes indicated on second and third frames. If desired, secure bow with a small amount of glue.

6. Center photos and lightweight cardboard behind photo openings. Glue photos to cardboard, then glue cardboard to frames. ❁

COLOR KEY	
Worsted Weight Yarn	**Yards**
▨ Dark denim #8793	25
▢ Rose #8921	3
▧ Arbutus #8922	3
▢ Winter white #8941	30
⟋ Light sea green #8878 Backstitch	1
⟋ Arbutus #8922 Backstitch	
○ Rose #8921 French Knot	
● Arbutus #8922 French Knot	
● Attach ribbon	
Color numbers given are for Spinrite Bernat Berella "4" worsted weight yarn.	

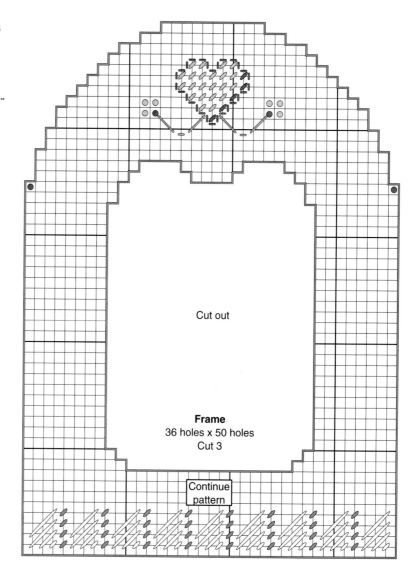

Cut out

Frame
36 holes x 50 holes
Cut 3

Continue pattern

Mother's Day   Mother's Day   Mother's Day   Mother's Day   Mother's Day

LAZY DAISIES
Mug

Design by Vicki Blizzard

Treat Mom to this colorful mug along with a box of her favorite tea for a special gift that will always make her think of you!

Skill Level: Beginner

Finished Size

Fits in a 3¼"-diameter acrylic mug with insert.

Materials

- ½ sheet Uniek Quick-Count 7-count plastic canvas
- Uniek Needloft plastic canvas yarn as listed in color key
- DMC 6-strand embroidery floss as listed in color key
- #16 tapestry needle
- Crafter's Pride red Mugs Your Way #30160RD acrylic mug with insert area from Daniel Enterprises

Instructions

1. Cut plastic canvas according to graph.

2. Stitch insert following graph. When background stitching is completed, work Lazy Daisy Stitches and French Knots with 6-strand embroidery floss over each square of white Continental Stitches as in Fig. 1.

3. With Christmas red, Whipstitch side edges together forming a tube; Overcast top and bottom edges.

4. Remove red insert from mug and place stitched tube in mug so that seam is at handle. Replace red insert inside stitched tube and snap firmly in place.

5. Remove stitched insert before washing. ❁

**Fig. 1
Embroidery**

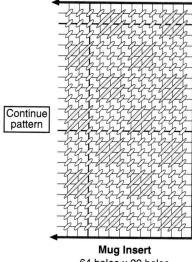

Continue pattern

Mug Insert
64 holes x 22 holes
Cut 1

COLOR KEY	
Plastic Canvas Yarn	**Yards**
☐ White #41	13
☐ Yellow #57	13
╱ Christmas red #02 Overcasting and Whipstitching	3
6-Strand Embroidery Floss	
⌀ Dark coral #349 Lazy Daisy	16
◎ Topaz #725 French Knot	4
Color numbers given are for Uniek Needloft plastic canvas yarn and DMC 6-strand embroidery floss.	

GARDEN TRELLIS
Clock

Design by Celia Lange Designs

Your mother will enjoy dressing up her bureau or vanity with this pretty garden trellis clock.

Skill Level: Intermediate

Finished Size
9¼" W x 5⅝" H x 1½" D

Materials
- 1 sheet Darice Ultra Stiff clear 7-count plastic canvas
- 1 sheet white 7-count plastic canvas yarn
- ¼ vertical sheet clear 7-count plastic canvas
- Coats & Clark Red Heart Super Saver worsted weight yarn Art. E300 and Art. E301 as listed in color key

- #16 tapestry needle
- 1½"-diameter battery-operated mini-clock Mini Bezel Arabic #908 from Walnut Hollow
- Assorted small silk flowers and leaves
- Small piece white STYRO-FOAM® brand plastic foam
- Hot-glue gun

Cutting & Stitching
1. Cut garden, clock pedestal and planter box pieces from stiff clear plastic canvas; cut trellis edges from regular clear plastic canvas according to graphs (pages 58 and 59).

2. Cut trellis from white plastic canvas following graph (page 58). Trellis will remain unstitched.

3. Stitch remaining pieces following graphs, working uncoded area on garden with light periwinkle Continental Stitches and uncoded area on clock pedestal with soft white Continental Stitches.

4. When background stitching is completed, Overcast all

Mother's Day   Mother's Day   Mother's Day   Mother's Day   Mother's Day

pedestal edges with Aran, bottom edge of garden with paddy green and inside edges of garden with light periwinkle.

5. Embroider vines on pedestal with grass green, then work French Knots on pedestal and garden with cornmeal, raspberry and light raspberry.

Assembly

1. Using white throughout assembly, Overcast outer and inner trellis edges, left and right ends of trellis and top edges of planter box sides.

2. Whipstitch two planter box long sides to two planter box short sides, then Whipstitch sides to one planter box bottom.

Repeat with remaining planter box pieces.

3. Whipstitch one long diagonal edge of trellis around sides and top of garden. Glue one outer trellis edge to top of trellis along back edge and garden edge, making sure edges are even.

4. Glue remaining outer trellis edge to top of trellis along front edge and inner trellis edge to inside of trellis along front edge, making edges protrude slightly beyond trellis.

5. Using photo as a guide, cut plastic foam to fit planter boxes; glue in place. Glue leaves and flowers in boxes.

6. Glue clock pedestal to

garden, aligning holes for clock. Glue boxes to sides of trellis, using boxes to level trellis if necessary.

7. Insert clock into hole, but do not glue in place. Clock should be removable to change battery. ❁

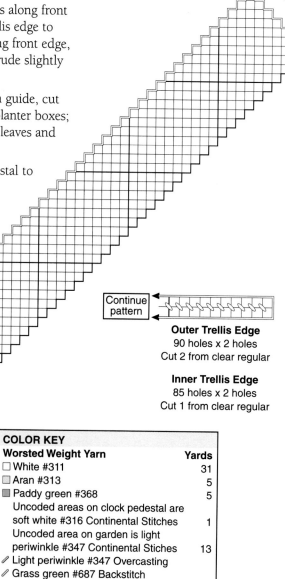

Right E

Continue pattern

Outer Trellis Edge
90 holes x 2 holes
Cut 2 from clear regular

Inner Trellis Edge
85 holes x 2 holes
Cut 1 from clear regular

Left End

Trellis
70 holes x 70 holes
Cut 1 from white

COLOR KEY	
Worsted Weight Yarn	**Yards**
☐ White #311	31
☐ Aran #313	5
◼ Paddy green #368	5
Uncoded areas on clock pedestal are soft white #316 Continental Stitches	1
Uncoded area on garden is light periwinkle #347 Continental Stiches	13
✎ Light periwinkle #347 Overcasting	
✎ Grass green #687 Backstitch and Straight Stitch	1
○ Cornmeal #320 French Knot	1
● Raspberry #368 French Knot	1
◉ Light raspberry #774 French Knot	1
Color numbers given are for Red Heart Super Saver worsted weight yarn Art. E300 and Art. E301.	

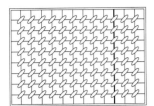

Planter Box Bottom
13 holes x 9 holes
Cut 2 from clear stiff

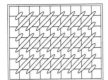

Planter Box Short Side
9 holes x 7 holes
Cut 4 from clear stiff

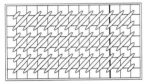

Planter Box Long Side
13 holes x 7 holes
Cut 4 from clear stiff

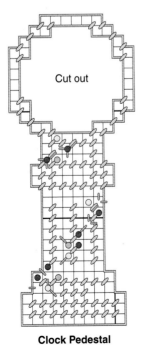

Clock Pedestal
12 holes x 29 holes
Cut 1 from clear stiff

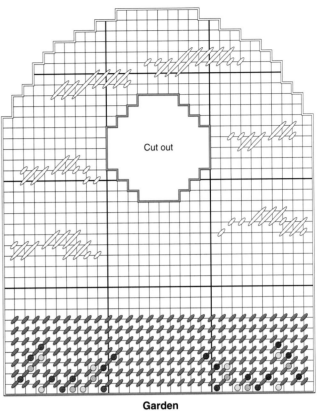

Cut out

Garden
30 holes x 36 holes
Cut 1 from clear stiff

COLOR KEY	
Worsted Weight Yarn	**Yards**
☐ White #311	31
☐ Aran #313	5
■ Paddy green #368	5
Uncoded areas on clock pedestal are soft white #316 Continental Stitches	1
Uncoded area on garden is light periwinkle #347 Continental Stiches	13
╱ Light periwinkle #347 Overcasting	
╱ Grass green #687 Backstitch and Straight Stitch	1
○ Cornmeal #320 French Knot	1
● Raspberry #368 French Knot	1
● Light raspberry #774 French Knot	1

Color numbers given are for Red Heart Super Saver worsted weight yarn Art. E300 and Art. E301.

Mother's Day   Mother's Day   Mother's Day   Mother's Day   Mother's Day

MAMA'S SLEEPING
Door Hanger

Design by Vicki Blizzard

Mother's Day   Mother's Day   Mother's Day   Mother's Day   Mother's Day

Please a mother with young children with this sweet door hanger.
She's sure to appreciate it!

Skill Level: Beginner

Finished Size

6⅛" W x 6¼" H excluding hanger ribbon

Materials

❀ 1 sheet Uniek Quick-Count 7-count plastic canvas

❀ Coats & Clark Red Heart Classic worsted weight yarn Art. E267 as listed in color key

❀ DMC #3 pearl cotton as listed in color key

❀ #16 tapestry needle

❀ 24" ⅜"-wide white picot-edge satin ribbon

❀ Hot-glue gun

Cutting & Stitching

1. Cut plastic canvas according to graphs (below and page 62).

2. Stitch pieces following graphs, working uncoded area on sign

with white Continental Stitches.

3. Whipstitch dart together on each ear with lily pink. Overcast ear with silver and sign with medium coral. Overcast all remaining pieces with adjacent colors.

4. When background stitching and Overcasting are completed, work yellow French Knot centers on flowers, lily pink French Knot for nose and paddy green Straight Stitches on leaves with 4 plies yarn.

5. Work country red letters on sign and lily pink Backstitches and Straight Stitches on hand and muzzle with 2 plies yarn. Backstitch eyes on head with black pearl cotton.

Assembly

1. Use photo as a guide throughout assembly. Glue strawberry caps to tops of two large strawberries. Glue muzzle

and ears to mouse head.

2. Evenly space and glue fence posts to fronts of fence rails. Arrange mouse, strawberries, leaves, flowers and mouse hand, then glue together and to left front of fence.

3. Cut an 8" length of silver yarn and tie a knot in one end. Glue knot to back of one large strawberry for mouse tail. Cut tail to desired length and tie a knot in end to prevent raveling.

4. Cut a 6" length of black pearl cotton. Thread ends from back to front through top corners of "DO NOT DISTURB" sign. Tie ends in a knot on front.

5. Cut a 16" length of white ribbon and glue ends to top back corners of top fence rail. Tie remaining ribbon in a bow and glue to front of ribbon hanger.

6. Hang "DO NOT DISTURB" sign over mouse hand. ❀

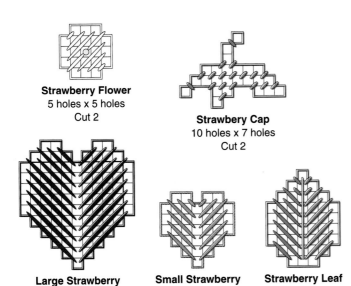

Strawberry Flower
5 holes x 5 holes
Cut 2

Strawbery Cap
10 holes x 7 holes
Cut 2

Large Strawberry
11 holes x 12 holes
Cut 3

Small Strawberry
7 holes x 7 holes
Cut 2

Strawberry Leaf
7 holes x 9 holes
Cut 3

COLOR KEY	
Worsted Weight Yarn	**Yards**
☐ White #1	24
▨ Medium coral #252	3
▨ Silver #412	4
▨ Paddy green #686	6
☐ Lily pink #719	1
■ Country red #914	5
Uncoded background on sign is white #1 Continental Stitches	
⁄ Paddy green #686 Straight Stitch	
⁄ Lily pink #719 Backstitch and Straight Stitch	
⁄ Country red #914 Backstitch	¼
○ Yellow #230 French Knot	
○ Lily pink #719 French Knot	
#3 Pearl Cotton	¼
⁄ Black #310 Backstitch	
Color numbers given are for Red Heart Classic worsted weight yarn Art. E267 and DMC #3 pearl cotton.	

Mother's Day   Mother's Day   Mother's Day   Mother's Day   Mother's Day

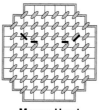

Mouse Head
9 holes x 9 holes
Cut 1

Join

Mouse Ear
5 holes x 5 holes
Cut 2

Mouse Muzzle
5 holes x 5 holes
Cut 1

Mouse Hand
5 holes x 4 holes
Cut 1

Fence Rail
40 holes x 7 holes
Cut 2

Fence Post
7 holes x 40 holes
Cut 3

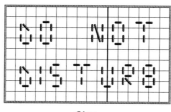

Sign
16 holes x 9 holes
Cut 1

COLOR KEY

Worsted Weight Yarn	Yards
☐ White #1	24
▨ Medium coral #252	3
☐ Silver #412	4
■ Paddy green #686	6
▨ Lily pink #719	1
■ Country red #914	5
Uncoded background on sign is white #1 Continental Stitches	
⁄ Paddy green #686 Straight Stitch	
⁄ Lily pink #719 Backstitch and Straight Stitch	
⁄ Country red #914 Backstitch	¼
○ Yellow #230 French Knot	
◉ Lily pink #719 French Knot	
#3 Pearl Cotton	¼
⁄ Black #310 Backstitch	

Color numbers given are for Red Heart Classic worsted weight yarn Art. E267 and DMC #3 pearl cotton.

Mother's Day   Mother's Day   Mother's Day   Mother's Day   Mother's Day

MOTHER'S GARDEN
Photo Frames

Design by Vicki Blizzard

Delight Mom with this unique photo display! It's just the right size for placing in a bright, sunny window!

Skill Level: Beginner

Finished Size
10⅜" W x 14" H x 4⅜" D

Materials
- 1 sheet Uniek Quick-Count 7-count plastic canvas
- Uniek Needloft plastic canvas yarn as listed in color key
- #16 tapestry needle
- 3½" x 4" x 10" basswood carving block #4112 from Walnut Hollow Farm Inc.
- Slender 3"-long nail
- Hammer
- 5 (18") lengths 18-gauge white-wrapped stem wire
- 12" 1"-diameter wooden dowel
- Fine sandpaper
- Wet paper towel
- Delta Ceramcoat acrylic paints: Christmas green #2068 Hunter green #2471
- Delta Ceramcoat Crackle aged cracked finish
- Delta Ceramcoat satin interior varnish
- 1" paintbrush
- Wood glue

Mother's Day   Mother's Day   Mother's Day   Mother's Day   Mother's Day

* 4" x 10" piece kelly green felt
* Hot-glue gun

Project Note

Stitch one flower photo frame for each photo up to five. Each flower takes 6 yards yellow, 7 yards white and 1 yard Christmas red. Each heart takes 2 yards Christmas red. Amounts given in color key are for sample model.

Instructions

1. Cut and stitch plastic canvas according to graphs.

2. Overcast outside edges of flowers with adjacent colors. Using Christmas red throughout, Overcast hearts, top and bottom edges of block strips and inside edges of flower fronts. Whipstitch short edges of block strips together, forming a rectangle.

3. For each flower, place one poinsettia front on one poinsettia back so that petals on front are centered between petals on back.

Carefully and gently pull white petals between yellow petals, placing small photo between layers before pulling last petal through. Cup flower in palm of one hand to shape.

Block Preparation

1. Without removing plastic from basswood block and using hammer and slender nail, make three holes in back row and two holes in front row, each approximately 2" deep. Remove plastic.

2. One at a time, wrap 18-gauge wires around 1" dowel, leaving 2" at each end uncoiled. Slide coils off dowel and stretch to shape, so there are three longer wires and two shorter wires.

3. Apply a large drop of glue on one end of each wire and insert in holes in block, placing longer wires in back and shorter wires in front. Allow to dry thoroughly.

4. Sand block to remove any rough spots. Wipe away sanding

residue with wet paper towel. Paint block and coiled stem wires with two coats Christmas green paint, allowing to dry thoroughly between coats.

5. Following manufacturer's instructions, apply one coat of crackle finish to block.

6. Apply one thin coat of hunter green paint to block, brushing gently in different directions. Allow to dry and crack.

7. Apply two coats of satin interior varnish block, drying thoroughly between coats.

8. Glue felt to block bottom. Allow to dry. Trim as necessary.

Final Assembly

1. Slide assembled stitched block strips over block. Center on block sides and glue in place.

2. Glue tops of wires in back row to backs of assembled flower photos. Glue tops of wires in front row to backs of stitched hearts. ✿

Heart
13 holes x 14 holes
Cut 2

COLOR KEY	
Plastic Canvas Yarn	**Yards**
■ Christmas red #02	25
□ White #41	20
□ Yellow #57	33
Color numbers given are for Uniek Needloft plastic canvas yarn.	

Continue pattern

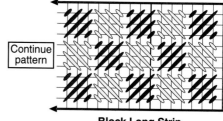

Block Long Strip
67 holes x 10 holes
Cut 2

Block Short Strip
28 holes x 10 holes
Cut 2

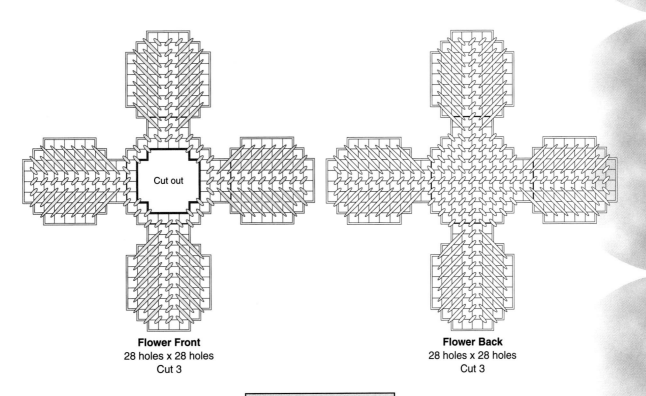

Flower Front
28 holes x 28 holes
Cut 3

Flower Back
28 holes x 28 holes
Cut 3

COLOR KEY	
Plastic Canvas Yarn	**Yards**
■ Christmas red #02	25
□ White #41	20
□ Yellow #57	33
Color numbers given are for Uniek Needloft plastic canvas yarn.	

Mother's Day   Mother's Day   Mother's Day   Mother's Day   Mother's Day

DAD'S DRESSER
Box

Design by Vicki Blizzard

**Dad will enjoy having this attractive dresser box
for placing loose change and other odds and ends.**

Skill Level: Beginner

Finished Size
Stitched Design: 5¾" square
Box: 7" square x 2½" H

Materials
- ½ sheet Uniek Quick-Count 7-count plastic canvas
- Honeysuckle Yarns rayon chenille yarn from Elmore-Pisgah Inc. as listed in color key
- #16 tapestry needle
- 7" oak box with 5¼" x 5¼" design area on lid from Sudberry House
- 9" x 12" sheet navy velveteen paper #P452 from Paper Adventures
- Small amount polyester fiberfill
- Tacky glue

Project Note
Yarn is doubled for stitching. For ease in stitching and to prevent yarn from excessive fraying, cut in 2-yard lengths. Thread end of one length through needle and pull until ends are even, then stitch with double thickness.

Instructions
1. Cut plastic canvas according to graph (page 68).
2. Stitch piece following graph and project note. Stitch center of design with a ruby Waffle Stitch (Fig. 1). Do not Overcast edges.
3. Bend back framer points on inside of lid and remove mounting board. Cut two pieces of navy velveteen paper the same size as the mounting board.
4. Glue one piece to backside of mounting board. Trim remaining piece as necessary to fit inside box bottom. Glue in place.
5. Place stitched insert in design area on lid. Evenly spread a handful of fiberfill over wrong side of insert. Place white side of mounting board next to fiberfill and bend framer points down to hold in place.

Fig. 1
Waffle Stitch

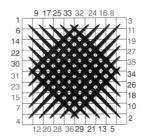

COLOR KEY	
Rayon Chenille Yarn	**Yards**
☐ Ivory #3	12
■ Sapphire #14	14
■ Ruby #23	18
Color numbers given are for Honeysuckle Yarns rayon chenille yarn.	

Father's Day   Father's Day   Father's Day

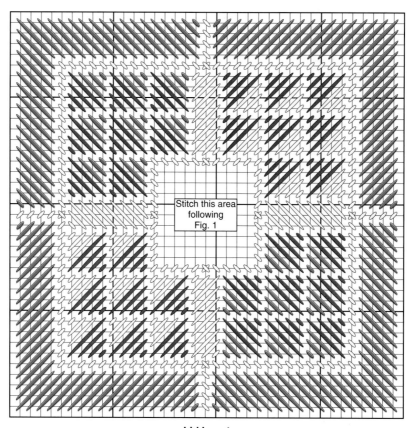

Stitch this area
following
Fig. 1

Lid Insert
38 holes x 38 holes
Cut 1

COLOR KEY	
Rayon Chenille Yarn	**Yards**
☐ Ivory #3	12
▨ Sapphire #14	14
■ Ruby #23	18
Color numbers given are for Honeysuckle Yarns rayon chenille yarn.	

SUNDAY
Sails Mug

Design by Vicki Blizzard

Whether the man of the house owns a boat or just dreams of sunny days on the water, he's sure to enjoy this colorful mug!

Skill Level: Beginner

Finished Size

Fits in a 3¼"-diameter acrylic mug with insert.

Materials

- ½ sheet Uniek Quick-Count 7-count plastic canvas
- Uniek Needloft plastic canvas yarn as listed in color key

- #16 tapestry needle
- Crafter's Pride white Mugs Your Way #30160W acrylic mug with insert area from Daniel Enterprises

Instructions

1. Cut and stitch plastic canvas according to graph (page 74).

2. Using sail blue, Whipstitch side edges together forming a tube;

Overcast top and bottom edges.

3. Remove white insert from mug and place stitched tube in mug so that seam is at handle. Replace white insert inside stitched tube and snap firmly in place.

4. Remove stitched insert before washing.

Continued on page 74

GONE FISHIN'
Door Hanger

Design by Vicki Blizzard

Outdoor sportsmen of all ages will appreciate and use this clever door hanger!

Skill Level: Beginner

Finished Size

6¾" W x 13¾" H

Materials

- 1 sheet Uniek Quick-Count 7-count plastic canvas
- ½ vertical sheet pastel green Uniek Quick-Count 7-count plastic canvas
- Uniek Needloft plastic canvas yarn as listed in color key
- DMC #3 pearl cotton as listed in color key
- #16 tapestry needle
- 1 yard 8-pound test monofilament fishing line
- Hot-glue gun

Instructions

1. Cut hanger front, fish, fishing rod, reel and reel handle from clear plastic canvas; cut hanger back from pastel green plastic canvas according to graphs (below, right and on page 72). Hanger back will remain unstitched.

2. Stitch hanger front following graph. Whipstitch hanger front to hanger back with light aqua.

3. Stitch and Overcast remaining pieces following graphs. Do not Overcast the three "loops" on bottom of rod. Work black pearl cotton French Knots on fish when background stitching is completed.

4. Using photo as a guide through step 9, glue letters to hanger front.

5. Cut a 12" length of fishing line and secure to bottom backside of fishing rod handle. Thread line through unstitched loops on bottom of rod. Glue fishing rod to hanger front.

6. Thread fishing line from front to back through hole indicated on one fish. Adjust line to desired length and secure on backside of fish; glue fish to hanger front.

7. Glue another fish between fishing rod and letters on top. Glue reel handle to reel, then glue reel to rod handle.

8. Thread remaining fishing line through last loop on fishing rod and tie in a knot at loop.

9. Thread ends of line from front to back through hole indicated on remaining two fish. Adjust lines to desired length and secure on backside of fish. Glue fish to hanger front.

Door Hanger Letters

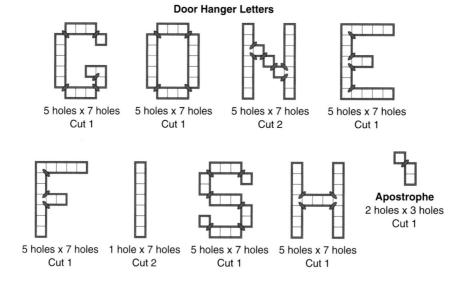

5 holes x 7 holes
Cut 1

5 holes x 7 holes
Cut 1

5 holes x 7 holes
Cut 2

5 holes x 7 holes
Cut 1

5 holes x 7 holes
Cut 1

1 hole x 7 holes
Cut 2

5 holes x 7 holes
Cut 1

5 holes x 7 holes
Cut 1

Apostrophe
2 holes x 3 holes
Cut 1

Fishing Rod
55 holes x 3 holes
Cut 1

Father's Day   Father's Day   Father's Day   Father's Day   Father's Day   Father's

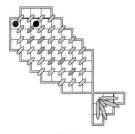

Fish
11 holes x 11 holes
Cut 4

Reel Handle
4 holes x 2 holes
Cut 1

Reel
4 holes x 4 holes
Cut 1

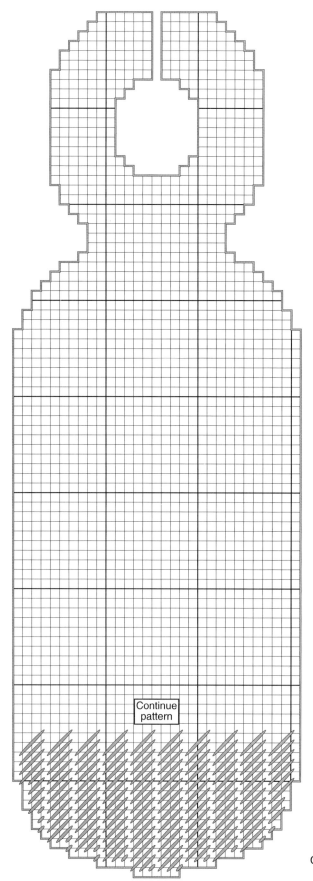

COLOR KEY

Plastic Canvas Yarn	Yards
☐ Pink #07	1
■ Maple #13	2
☐ Tan #18	1
☐ Mint #24	3
☐ Moss #25	2
■ Forest #29	5
☐ Light aqua #49	46

#3 Pearl Cotton

● Black #310 French Knot	1
● Attach fishing line	

Color numbers given are for Uniek Needloft plastic canvas yarn.

Continue pattern

Door Hanger Front & Back
31 holes x 90 holes
Cut 1 from clear for front
Stitch as graphed
Cut 1 from pastel green for back
Do not stitch

LOG CABIN
Coaster Set

Design by Laura Scott

Stitch this handsome coaster set for Dad to enjoy during quiet evenings in the den.

Skill Level: Beginner

Finished Size

Coaster: 3⅞" square

Coaster Box: 4¼" square x 1¾" H

Materials

- 1 sheet 7-count plastic canvas
- Uniek Needloft plastic canvas yarn as listed in color key
- #16 tapestry needle
- 9" x 12" sheet cocoa brown self-adhesive Presto felt from Kunin Felt

Instructions

1. Cut plastic canvas according to graphs (page 74). Cut one 27-hole x 27-hole piece for coaster box base. Base will remain unstitched.

2. Cut one piece of felt to fit each coaster, bottom of base and top of base inside box. Set aside.

3. Stitch pieces following graphs. Alternating yarn colors maple and brown, Overcast coasters and top edges of box sides. With maple, Whipstitch box sides together, then Whipstitch sides to unstitched base.

4. Adhere felt to wrong sides of coasters, to bottom of base and to base inside box.

her's Day   Father's Day   Father's Day   Father's Day   Father's Day   Father's Day

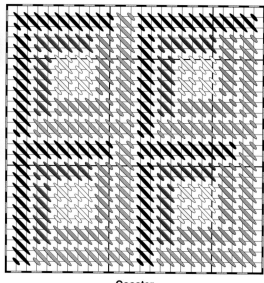

Coaster
25 holes x 25 holes
Cut 4

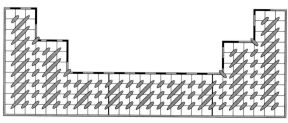

COLOR KEY	
Plastic Canvas Yarn	**Yards**
■ Burgundy #03	7
■ Maple #13	24
■ Brown #15	15
☐ Gold #17	2
■ Forest #29	6
☐ Camel #43	2
Color numbers given are for Uniek Needloft plastic canvas yarn.	

Box Side
27 holes x 10 holes
Cut 4

Sunday Sails

Continued from page 69

COLOR KEY	
Plastic Canvas Yarn	**Yards**
■ Christmas red #02	1
■ Maple #13	1
■ Fern #23	1
■ Sail blue #35	20
☐ White #41	2
☐ Yellow #57	1
■ Purple #46	1
Color numbers given are for Uniek Needloft plastic canvas yarn.	

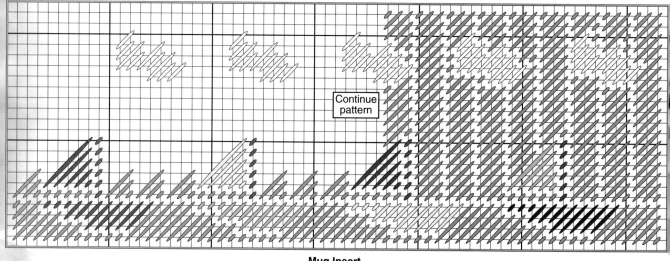

Continue pattern

Mug Insert
64 holes x 23 holes
Cut 1

I LOVE DAD
Desk Marker

Design by Judi Kauffman

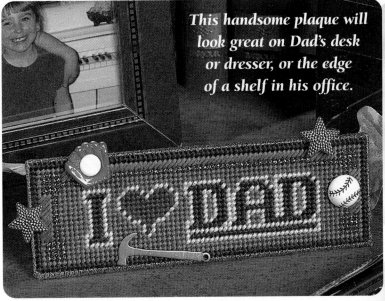

This handsome plaque will look great on Dad's desk or dresser, or the edge of a shelf in his office.

Skill Level: Beginner

Size

5⅛" W x 1¾" H excluding buttons

Materials

- 14-count green plastic canvas
- 6-strand embroidery floss as listed in color key
- Medium (#16) braid as listed in color key
- 1/16" ribbon as listed in color key
- Old scissors or wire cutters
- Novelty buttons: baseball mitt, baseball and 2 gold stars
- Hammer-shaped brass charm
- Tacky craft glue
- Paper towels

Instructions

1. Referring to graph, cut plastic canvas. Cut also one piece 71 holes x 16 holes for bottom; it will remain unstitched.

2. Using 6 strands floss and one strand medium (#16) braid, stitch design as shown.

3. Using green metallic 1/16" ribbon throughout, Overcast short ends of stitched front and unstitched back. Whipstitch front to back, back to bottom and bottom to front.

4. Put on protective glasses. Using old scissors, carefully snap shanks off backs of decorative buttons; discard pieces carefully to protect children and pets.

5. Prop stitched plaque between crumpled paper towels so stitched surface can lie flat as glue dries. Referring to photo, glue buttons and charm in place; let dry completely.

COLOR KEY	
6-Strand Embroidery Floss	**Yards**
■ Green #245	8
■ Rust #341	1
■ Dark brown #382	4
☐ Off-white #390	4
Uncoded areas are green #245 Continental Stitches	
Medium (#16) Braid	
☐ Copper hi-lustre #021 HL	3
1/16" Ribbon	
⁄ Green #008 Overcasting	3
Color numbers given are for Anchor 6-strand embroidery floss from Coats & Clark and Kreinik Medium (#16) Braid and 1/16" Ribbon.	

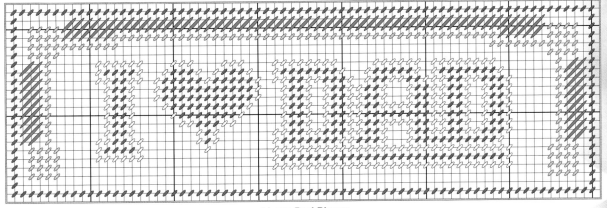

I Love Dad Plaque
71 holes x 23 holes
Cut 2, stitch 1

her's Day   Father's Day   Father's Day   Father's Day   Father's Day   Father's Day

UNCLE SAM
Teddy Bear

Design by Angie Arickx

*Decorate your door during the summer months
with this all-American, Uncle Sam teddy bear!*

Skill Level: Beginner

Finished Size

10⅛" W x 9⅝" H

Materials

★ 1 sheet 7-count plastic canvas

★ Uniek Needloft plastic canvas yarn as listed in color key

★ #16 tapestry needle

Instructions

1. Cut plastic canvas according to graph.

2. Stitch piece following graph, working uncoded areas with dark royal Continental Stitches. Work Backstitches when background stitching is completed.

3. Overcast edges following graph.

4. Hang as desired. ★

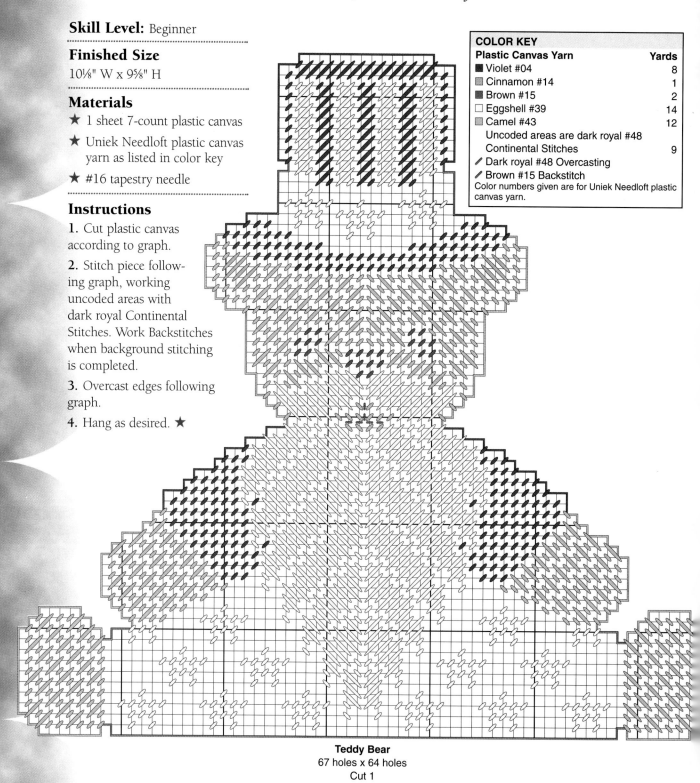

COLOR KEY		
Plastic Canvas Yarn		**Yards**
■ Violet #04		8
▨ Cinnamon #14		1
■ Brown #15		2
□ Eggshell #39		14
▨ Camel #43		12
Uncoded areas are dark royal #48		
Continental Stitches		9
╱ Dark royal #48 Overcasting		
╱ Brown #15 Backstitch		
Color numbers given are for Uniek Needloft plastic canvas yarn.		

Teddy Bear
67 holes x 64 holes
Cut 1

Fourth of July   Fourth of July   Fourth of July   Fourth of July   Fourth of July

PATRIOTIC
Welcome

Design by Robin Petrina

Invite guests into your home with this red, white and blue welcome sign!

Skill Level: Beginner

Finished Size

12¼" W x 7" H

Materials

★ 1 sheet 7-count plastic canvas

★ Metallic craft cord as listed in color key

★ Hot-glue gun

Instructions

1. Cut plastic canvas according to graphs (pages 79 and 80).

2. Stitch pieces following graphs, working uncoded background on stars with white pearl Continental Stitches. Work red/silver Backstitches and white pearl Straight Stitches on stars when background stitching is completed.

3. Overcast banner and stars with blue/silver and "WEL-COME" with red/silver.

4. Using photo as a guide through step 6, cut seven 3"–4" lengths of red/silver cord. Thread lengths from front to back through holes indicated on banner. Knot on backside.

5. Thread remaining ends through hole indicated on each star, placing stars in order so they spell the word "FRIENDS." Adjust each to desired length, making the "F," "E" and "S" stars shorter than remaining stars; knot on backsides.

6. Center and glue "WELCOME" to banner front. Hang as desired. ★

Fourth of July   Fourth of July   Fourth of July   Fourth of July   Fourth of July

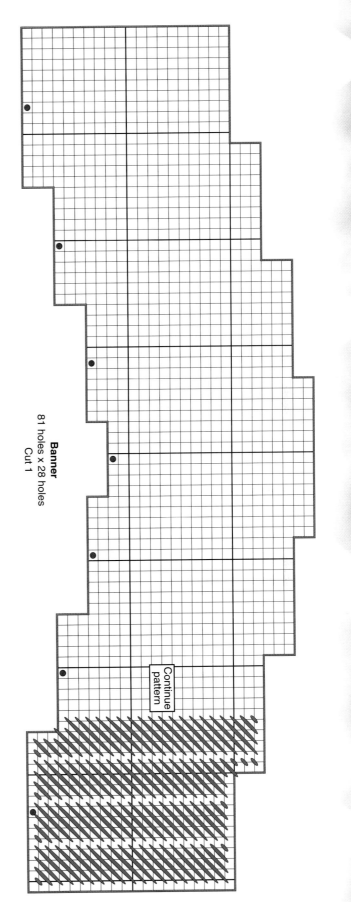

Banner
81 holes x 28 holes
Cut 1

Continue pattern

COLOR KEY

Metallic Craft Cord	Yards
▨ Blue/silver	28
☐ White pearl	13
▨ Red/silver	11

Uncoded areas are white pearl Continental Stitches

◿ White pearl Straight Stitch

◿ Red/silver Backstitch

● Attach red/silver hanger

Fourth of July   Fourth of July   Fourth of July   Fourth of July   Fourth of July

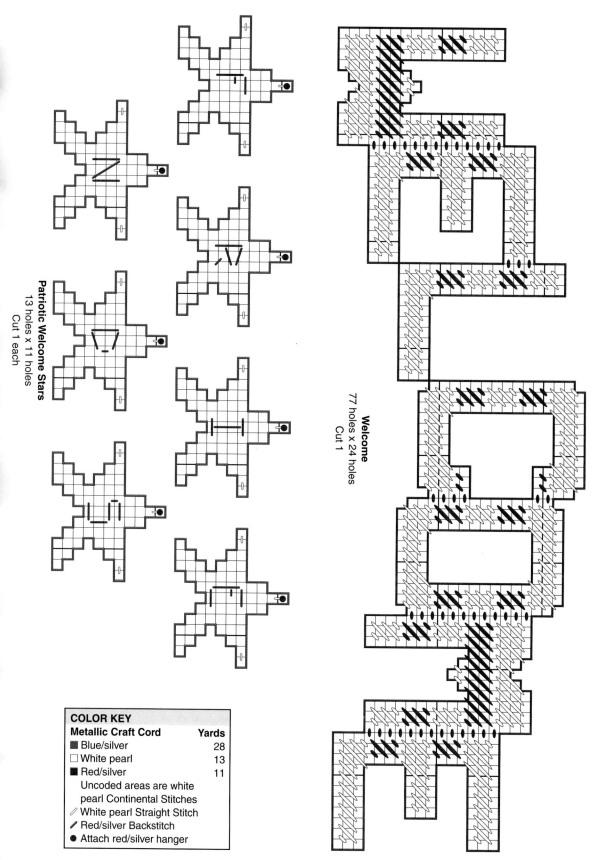

Patriotic Welcome Stars
13 holes x 11 holes
Cut 1 each

Welcome
77 holes x 24 holes
Cut 1

COLOR KEY
Metallic Craft Cord   Yards
■ Blue/silver   28
□ White pearl   13
■ Red/silver   11
 Uncoded areas are white
 pearl Continental Stitches
⁄ White pearl Straight Stitch
⁄ Red/silver Backstitch
● Attach red/silver hanger

STAR SPANGLED Star

Design by Kathleen J. Fischer

Stick this sparkly star in a window to show your pride in America!

Skill Level: Beginner

Finished Size

6¼" W x 6¼" H

Materials

★ 2 (5") plastic canvas star shapes by Uniek

★ Worsted weight yarn as listed in color key

★ #16 tapestry needle

★ 4 white star pony beads from The Beadery

★ 1¾" suction cup

★ 3 silver tinsel chenille stems

★ Pencil

★ Low-temperature glue gun

Instructions

1. Cut star back according to graph (page 82), cutting away gray area. Star back will remain unstitched.

2. Stitch star front following graph (page 82). Using blue yarn, attach pony beads to star where indicated on graphs.

3. Insert suction cup in bottom diamond opening on star back. Whipstitch wrong sides of star front and back together with red and blue following graphs.

4. Cut tinsel chenille stems into five 3" lengths and 10 (2") lengths. Using photo as guide, curl a few stems around pencil, then glue 15 stems to back of assembled star. ★

ourth of July   Fourth of July   Fourth of July   Fourth of July   Fourth of July

Star Spangled Star

Continued from previous page

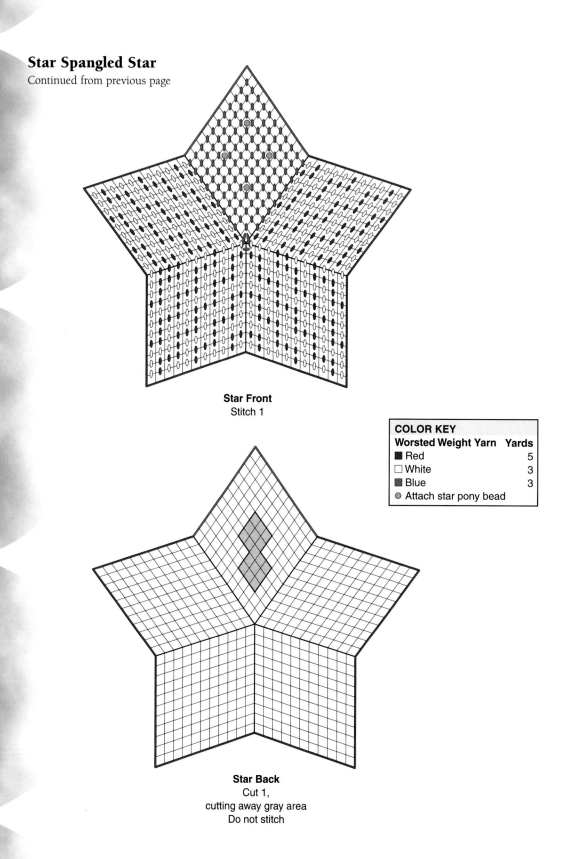

Star Front
Stitch 1

COLOR KEY

Worsted Weight Yarn	Yards
■ Red	5
□ White	3
■ Blue	3
● Attach star pony bead	

Star Back
Cut 1,
cutting away gray area
Do not stitch

CUPCAKE Pokes

Design by Vicki Blizzard

Stitch these quick and easy cupcake pokes to add a festive touch to this year's Fourth of July family reunion picnic!

Skill Level: Beginner

Finished Size

USA: 2⅜" W x 1¼" H excluding skewer

Rocket: 1¼" W x 4" H excluding skewer

Striped Heart: 2" W x 2" H excluding skewer

Blue Heart: 2" W x 2" H excluding skewer

Materials

★ Small amount 7-count plastic canvas

★ Coats & Clark Red Heart Classic worsted weight yarn Art. E267 as listed in color key

★ Kreinik ⅛" Ribbon as listed in color key

★ #16 tapestry needle

★ 4 (12") bamboo skewers

★ Hot-glue gun

Instructions

1. Cut plastic canvas according to graphs (page 88).

2. Stitch and Overcast pieces following graphs.

3. When stitching and Overcasting are completed, work soft navy and black Straight Stitches on rocket and white Straight Stitches on star using 4 plies. Work white Backstitches on rocket using 2 plies. Work Aztec gold ribbon Backstitches and Straight Stitches on USA letters.

4. Thread a 3" length of ⅛"-wide Aztec gold ribbon from front to back through hole indicated on rocket graph; secure on backside. Unravel ribbon to make fireworks trail.

5. Center and glue star to front of blue heart.

6. Trim skewers to desired length. Glue trimmed end of skewers to back of each stitched piece. ★

Continued on page 88

Fourth of July   Fourth of July   Fourth of July   Fourth of July   Fourth of July

ROCKET
Sam

Design by Janelle Giese

This delightful Uncle Sam is coming to your Fourth of July picnic in his very own rocket! Use him as an indoor or outdoor decoration!

Skill Level: Beginner

Finished Size

5" W x 13" H

Materials

★ ½ sheet 7-count plastic canvas

★ Uniek Needloft plastic canvas yarn as listed in color key

★ DMC #5 pearl cotton as listed in color key

★ Kreinik ⅛" Ribbon as listed in color key

★ #16 tapestry needle

★ Gold star garland

★ Thick white glue

Instructions

1. Cut plastic canvas according to graphs.

2. Stitch pieces following graphs, working uncoded areas with dark royal Continental Stitches.

3. Embroider stars on rocket with ⅛"-wide ribbon, working the horizontal stitch first, then the Cross Stitch on top. Work nose with red yarn and remaining embroidery with black pearl cotton, stitching each eye four times.

4. Overcast pieces following graphs.

5. Using photo as a guide, curl a length of star garland around a pencil. With pearl cotton, attach garland to center back of rocket top and to right side of head on rocket. Glue to secure.

6. For rocket fire, curl three lengths of star garland around a pencil. Form a cluster with curled garland at bottom of rocket and secure with black pearl cotton and glue. ★

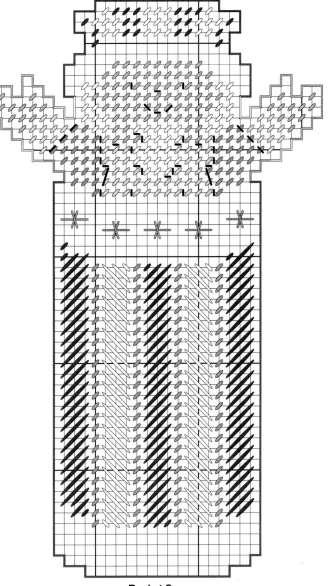

Rocket Sam
32 holes x 54 holes
Cut 1

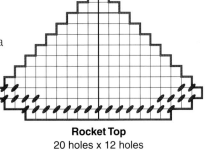

Rocket Top
20 holes x 12 holes
Cut 1

COLOR KEY	
Plastic Canvas Yarn	**Yards**
■ Red #01	6
▨ Royal #32	1
☐ Sail blue #35	2
☐ Beige #40	1
☐ White #41	4
▨ Flesh tone #56	3
Uncoded areas are dark royal #48 Continental Stitches	9
╱ Dark royal #48 Overcasting	
╱ Red #01 Backstitch	
⅛" Ribbon	
▨ Gold #002HL	2
╱ Gold #002HL Straight Stitch	
#5 Pearl Cotton	
╱ Black #310 Backstitch	2
Color numbers given are for Uniek Needloft plastic canvas yarn, Kreinik ⅛" Ribbon and DMC #5 pearl cotton.	

PATRIOTIC
Tissue Topper

Design by Angie Arickx

*Just the right size for a desktop or in your car,
this patriotic tissue topper is both handy and decorative.*

Skill Level: Beginner

Finished Size

Fits junior-size tissue box

Materials

★ 1 sheet Uniek Quick-Count 7-count plastic canvas

★ Uniek Needloft plastic canvas yarn as listed in color key

★ #16 tapestry needle

Instructions

1. Cut plastic canvas according to graphs.

2. Stitch pieces following graphs, Overcasting inside edges on top while stitching.

3. Using dark royal throughout,

Whipstitch sides together, then Whipstitch sides to top. Overcast bottom edges. ★

COLOR KEY	
Plastic Canvas Yarn	**Yards**
■ Violet #04	11
☐ Eggshell #39	22
■ Dark royal #48	20
Color numbers given are for Uniek Needloft plastic canvas yarn.	

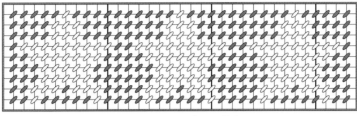

Tissue Topper Short Side
34 holes x 10 holes
Cut 2

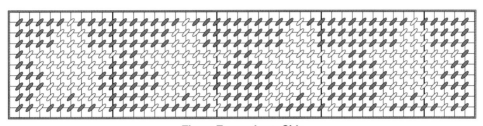

Tissue Topper Long Side
45 holes x 10 holes
Cut 2

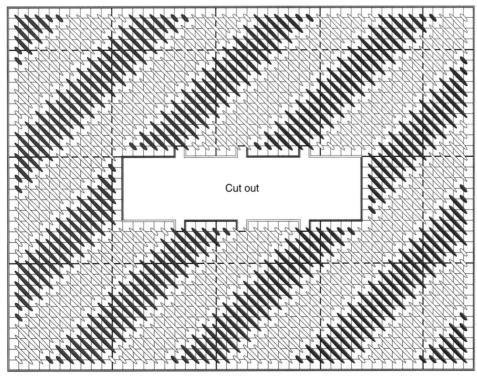

Cut out

Tissue Topper Top
45 holes x 34 holes
Cut 1

Cupcake Pokes

Continued from page 83

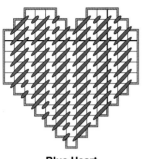

Blue Heart
13 holes x 13 holes
Cut 1

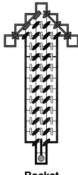

Rocket
7 holes x 15 holes
Cut 1

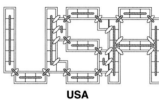

USA
15 holes x 7 holes
Cut 1

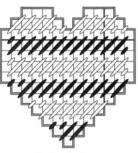

Striped Heart
13 holes x 13 holes
Cut 1

Star
5 holes x 6 holes
Cut 1

COLOR KEY	
Worsted Weight Yarn	**Yards**
☐ White #1	4
■ Soft navy #853	3
■ Cherry red #912	2
╱ Black #12 Straight Stitch and Overcasting	¼
╱ White #1 Backstitch and Straight Stitch	
╱ Soft navy #853 Straight Stitch	
⅛"-Wide Ribbon	
╱ Aztec gold #202HL Backstitch, Straight Stitch and Overcasting	3
● Attach fireworks trail	
Color numbers given are for Red Heart Classic worsted weight yarn Art. E267 and Kreinik ⅛" Ribbon.	

Fourth of July   Fourth of July   Fourth of July   Fourth of July   Fourth of Jul

HALLOWEEN
Wind Chimes

Designs by Joan Green

This whimsical pair of miniature wind chimes won't frighten anyone on Halloween, but they will add a colorful splash of color to your party decor!

Skill Level: Intermediate

Finished Size

Jack-o'-Lantern: Approximately 4¼" W x 14" H including hanger

Black Cat: Approximately 5½" W x 14" H including hanger

Materials

- 1 sheet 7-count plastic canvas
- Spinrite plastic canvas yarn as listed in color key
- Spinrite Bernat Berella "4" worsted weight yarn as listed in color key
- #16 tapestry needle
- 2 yards gold #2024 metallic embroidery thread Art. #9812 by Madeira Threads
- #24 tapestry needle
- 2 gold tinsel chenille stems
- Chenille stems: 1 each orange and yellow
- 4 (10mm) movable eyes
- 2 (5-piece) sets 6mm Craftwood gold steel mini wind chimes #1624-29 from Darice
- Needle-nose pliers (optional)
- Hot-glue gun

Cutting & Stitching

1. Cut plastic canvas according to graphs (page 91).

2. Using #16 tapestry needle, stitch pieces following graphs, reversing one jack-o'-lantern before stitching. When background stitching is completed, work tangelo Backstitches on both black cat faces.

3. Whipstitch wrong sides of two candy corn pieces together with adjacent colors. Repeat with remaining two candy corn pieces.

4. Matching edges and with wrong sides together, Whipstitch black cat pieces together and jack-o'-lantern pieces together following graphs. ***Note:*** *If desired, use needle-nose pliers to help pull yarn through tight places.*

Finishing

1. Use photo as a guide throughout assembly. Cut gold metallic embroidery thread in half.

2. Knot one end of one half. Using #24 tapestry needle, thread between two layers of canvas on cat near farthest left hole indicated for attaching chimes. Conceal knot on inside and bring thread through hole to front.

3. Thread on longest chime, leaving about ¾" between chime and bottom of cat; bring thread back through same hole to back piece. Continue threading on chimes in descending order through holes indicated, making sure tops of chimes are even.

4. After attaching last chime, bring thread through to back piece, make a small knot; trim excess.

5. Knot one end of excess thread, then thread other end through hole indicated with blue dot on one candy corn then through middle chime, leaving about ¾" between chime and candy corn. Tack thread over edge of candy corn several times to secure.

6. Repeat steps 2–5 for jack-o'-lantern with remaining half of metallic thread and last set of chimes.

7. Glue movable eyes to cat faces above noses. For whiskers, cut orange and yellow chenille stems into four 2½" pieces. Glue two orange and two yellow whiskers to one side of cat. Glue remaining orange and yellow whiskers to other side of cat.

8. Insert both ends of one gold tinsel chenille stem through top of cat, pushing 1" of ends between two layers of canvas. Secure at point of entry with a dab of glue.

9. Repeat with remaining gold tinsel chenille stem on jack-o'-lantern, inserting one end on each side of stem.

Halloween   Halloween   Halloween   Halloween   Halloween   Halloween

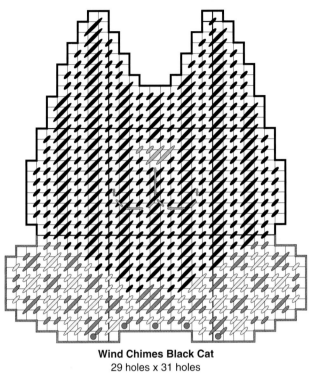

Wind Chimes Black Cat
29 holes x 31 holes
Cut 2

Wind Chimes Candy Corn
7 holes x 11 holes
Cut 4

COLOR KEY

Plastic Canvas Yarn	Yards
■ Orange #0030	22
Worsted Weight Yarn	
□ Sunshine #8701	10
▨ Tangelo #8704	8
▨ Light sea green #8878	1
□ White #8942	2
■ Black #8994	20

Uncoded areas on jack-o'-lantern are
tangelo #8704 Continental Stitches

∕ Tangelo #8704 Backstitch

● Attach chime

Color numbers given are for Spinrite plastic canvas yarn
and Spinrite Bernat Berella "4" worsted weight yarn.

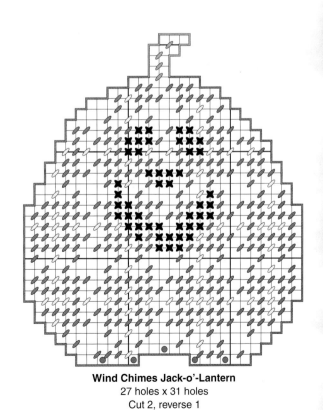

Wind Chimes Jack-o'-Lantern
27 holes x 31 holes
Cut 2, reverse 1

Halloween   Halloween   Halloween   Halloween   Halloween   Halloween

PUMPKIN
Greeting

Design by Janelle Giese

Greet friends and family into your home, or coworkers into your office, with this cheery greeting sign!

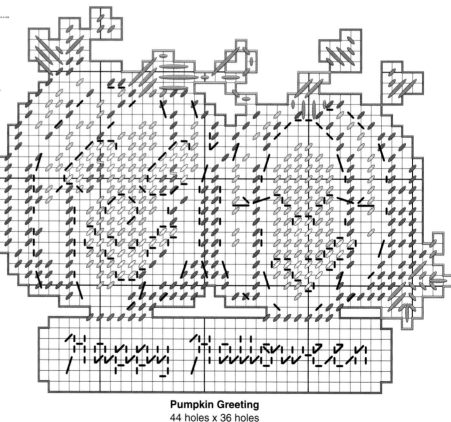

Skill Level: Intermediate

Finished Size

6¾" W x 5½" H

Materials

- ½ sheet 7-count plastic canvas
- Uniek Needloft plastic canvas yarn as listed in color key
- DMC 6-strand embroidery floss as listed in color key
- DMC #5 pearl cotton as listed in color key
- #16 tapestry needle

Instructions

1. Cut plastic canvas according to graph.

2. Stitch and Overcast piece following graph, working uncoded areas on pumpkin with pumpkin Continental

Stitches and uncoded areas on sign with yellow Continental Stitches.

3. Work ecru highlights on eyes of left pumpkin with 6-strands floss, stitching each three times.

4. Embroider words and remaining features on pumpkins with black pearl cotton, working each stitch of smiling eyes on right pumpkin three times.

5. Hang as desired. 🎃

COLOR KEY	
Plastic Canvas Yarn	**Yards**
■ Black #00	3
■ Rose #06	1
■ Rust #09	6
□ Tangerine #11	3
■ Avocado #30	2
□ Yellow #57	5
Uncoded areas are pumpkin #12 Continental Stitches	6
Uncoded area on sign is yellow #57 Continental Stitches	
#5 Pearl Cotton	
✎ Black #310 Backstitch and Straight Stitch	6
6-Strand Embroidery Floss	
✎ Ecru Straight Stitch	1
Color numbers given are for Uniek Needloft plastic canvas yarn and DMC #5 pearl cotton.	

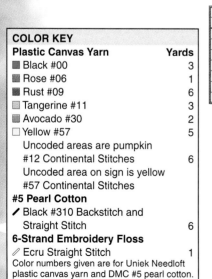

Pumpkin Greeting
44 holes x 36 holes
Cut 1

Halloween   Halloween   Halloween   Halloween   Halloween   Halloween

GHOSTS & GRAVES
Basket

Design by Celia Lange Designs

*Filled with candy corn or other treats, this creepy basket
makes a great decoration for a Halloween party!*

Skill Level: Beginner

Finished Size

9¼" W x 3" H x 5¾" D

Materials

- 2 sheets Darice Ultra Stiff 7-count plastic canvas
- Coats & Clark Red Heart Classic worsted weight yarn Art. E267 as listed in color key
- DMC #3 pearl cotton as listed in color key
- #16 tapestry needle
- 6 (1"–1½") miniature pumpkins
- Assorted miniature autumn leaves
- ½ sheet dark green Fun Foam craft foam by Westrim Crafts
- Hot-glue gun

Instructions

1. Cut plastic canvas according to graphs (pages 93–95).

2. Stitch pieces following graphs, reversing two ghosts before stitching. Overcast ghosts and gravestones with adjacent colors.

3. Embroider gravestones and ghost faces with black pearl cotton when background stitching and Overcasting are completed.

4. Using nickel throughout, Overcast two fence posts. Whipstitch two fence posts together along one long side; Overcast remaining edges. Repeat with remaining fence posts for a total of four corner posts.

Continued on page 95

COLOR KEY	
Worsted Weight Yarn	**Yards**
☐ White #1	14
■ Black #12	13
▨ Nickel #401	15
☐ Silver #412	6
▨ Medium sage #632	39
#3 Pearl Cotton	
╱ Black #310 Backstitch and Straight Stitch	2
● Black #310 French Knot	
Color numbers given are for Red Heart Classic worsted weight yarn Art. E267 and DMC #3 pearl cotton.	

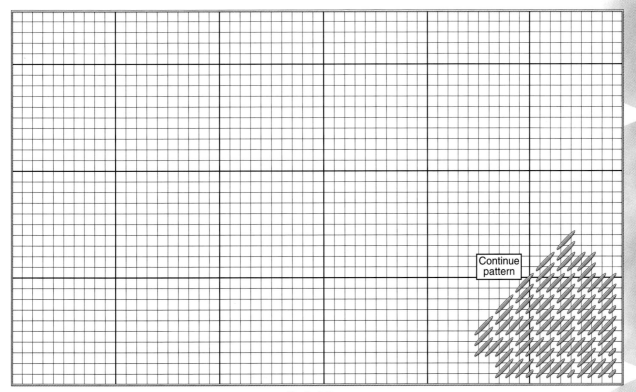

Basket Base
59 holes x 35 holes
Cut 1

Halloween   Halloween   Halloween   Halloween   Halloween   Halloween

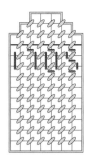

Dated Gravestone
7 holes x 13 holes
Cut 2

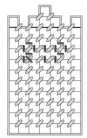

RIP Gravestone
7 holes x 12 holes
Cut 2

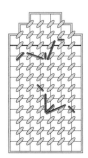

Bat Gravestone
7 holes x 13 holes
Cut 2

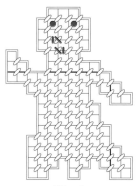

Ghost
12 holes x 16 holes
Cut 6, reverse 2

COLOR KEY	
Worsted Weight Yarn	**Yards**
☐ White #1	14
■ Black #12	13
▨ Nickel #401	15
☐ Silver #412	6
▨ Medium sage #632	39
#3 Pearl Cotton	
╱ Black #310 Backstitch	
and Straight Stitch	2
● Black #310 French Knot	

Color numbers given are for Red Heart Classic worsted weight yarn Art. E267 and DMC #3 pearl cotton.

5. Using adjacent colors throughout, Whipstitch top rails together along short edges and bottom rails together along short edges. Overcast top and bottom edges of fence rails.

6. Overcast base with medium sage. Trim dark green craft foam as necessary to fit base; glue to bottom side.

7. Using photo as guide through step 9, center and glue bottom rails to base. Glue corner posts in place, then glue top rails inside corner posts ½" above bottom rails.

8. Center and glue remaining two fence posts to fronts of long fence rails. Glue ghosts and tombstones to base, rails and posts.

9. Glue pumpkins and leaves to base. 🎃

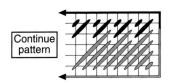

Long Bottom Fence Rail
49 holes x 6 holes
Cut 2
Short Bottom Fence Rail
25 holes x 6 holes
Cut 2

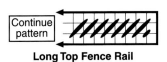

Long Top Fence Rail
49 holes x 3 holes
Cut 2
Short Top Fence Rail
25 holes x 3 holes
Cut 2

Fence Post
5 holes x 17 holes
Cut 10

COLOR KEY	
Worsted Weight Yarn	**Yards**
☐ White #1	14
■ Black #12	13
■ Nickel #401	15
☐ Silver #412	6
■ Medium sage #632	39
#3 Pearl Cotton	
╱ Black #310 Backstitch and Straight Stitch	2
● Black #310 French Knot	
Color numbers given are for Red Heart Classic worsted weight yarn Art. E267 and DMC #3 pearl cotton.	

Halloween   Halloween   Halloween   Halloween   Halloween   Halloween

HAUNTED GRAVESTONE
Memo Holder

Design by Judy Collishaw

**Keep those last-minute Halloween to-do notes close
at hand with this spooky memo pad holder!**

Skill Level: Beginner

Finished Size
6¼" W x 8½" H

Materials
- 🎃 1 sheet 7-count plastic canvas
- 🎃 Worsted weight yarn as listed in color key
- 🎃 DMC #3 pearl cotton as listed in color key
- 🎃 #16 tapestry needle
- 🎃 3 (1¼") round magnets
- 🎃 3" x 5" notepad with top spiral
- 🎃 Pencil
- 🎃 1" ¼"-wide white elastic
- 🎃 Sewing needle and white sewing thread
- 🎃 Low-temperature glue gun

Instructions

1. Cut plastic canvas according to graphs.

2. Stitch pieces following graphs, Overcasting inside edges indicated on memo holder while stitching. Do not stitch area under the cut out holes.

3. When background stitching is completed, work letters on gravestone with 2 plies black yarn. Work eyes and facial features with pearl cotton.

4. Using mustard throughout, Overcast top edge of broom bristles back with mustard. Matching edges and with wrong sides together, Whipstitch broom bristles front and back together; Overcast remaining edges of broom bristles front with adjacent colors.

5. Overcast bat and outside edges of memo holder following graphs.

6. With sewing needle and white thread, sew ¼"-wide elastic in a circle. Glue seam side of elastic to back of witch's wrist on right side of holder.

7. Using photo as a guide, glue bat to arm above gravestone.

Glue magnets to backside of face and skirt and to arm below bat.

8. Glue broom bristles to back of foot and skirt, making sure bottom edges are even. For broom handle, insert pencil through elastic into broom bristles.

9. Insert back of notepad through cut out holes. 🎃

Halloween   Halloween   Halloween   Halloween   Halloween   Halloween

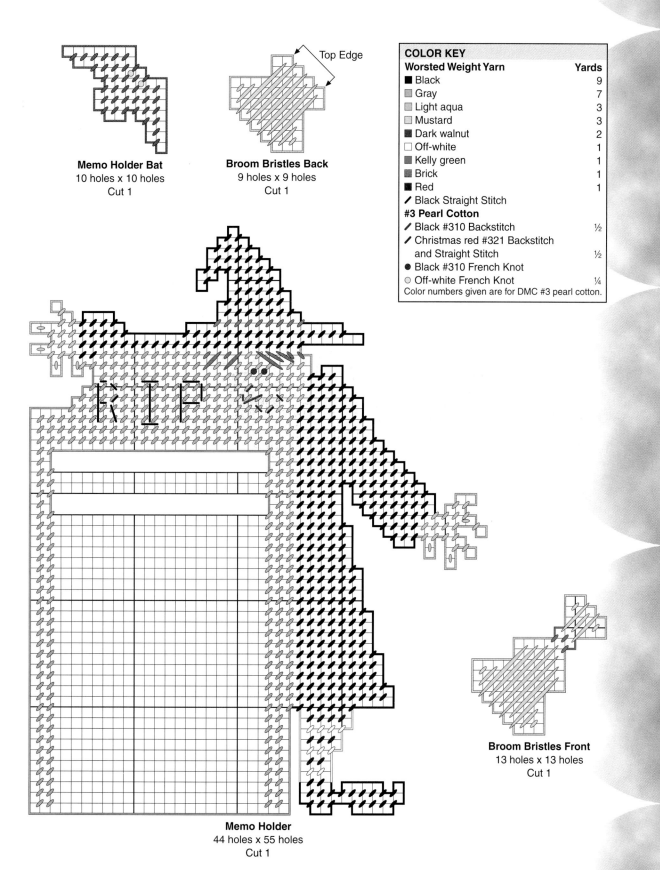

Memo Holder Bat
10 holes x 10 holes
Cut 1

Broom Bristles Back
9 holes x 9 holes
Cut 1

Top Edge

COLOR KEY

Worsted Weight Yarn	Yards
■ Black	9
▨ Gray	7
▨ Light aqua	3
▨ Mustard	3
▨ Dark walnut	2
☐ Off-white	1
▨ Kelly green	1
▨ Brick	1
■ Red	1
╱ Black Straight Stitch	

#3 Pearl Cotton

╱ Black #310 Backstitch	½
╱ Christmas red #321 Backstitch and Straight Stitch	½
● Black #310 French Knot	
○ Off-white French Knot	¼

Color numbers given are for DMC #3 pearl cotton.

Broom Bristles Front
13 holes x 13 holes
Cut 1

Memo Holder
44 holes x 55 holes
Cut 1

Halloween Halloween Halloween Halloween Halloween Halloween

CANDY CORN
Party Accents

Designs by Ronda Bryce

Whether your Halloween party guests are young or simply young at heart, they're sure to enjoy this colorful set of table accents!

Skill Level: Beginner

Finished Size
Basket: 3⅜" W x 5¾" H x 3⅜" D

Glass Holder: 3½" H x 3½" in diameter

Napkin Ring: 2⅜" W x 3½" H x 1¼" in diameter

Materials
- 1½ sheets 7-count plastic canvas
- 4½" plastic canvas radial circle by Darice
- Uniek Needloft plastic canvas yarn as listed in color key
- #16 tapestry needle

Instructions

1. Cut basket sides and handle, glass holder side and napkin ring pieces from plastic canvas according to graphs (pages 98 and 100). Cut one 21-hole x 21-hole piece from plastic canvas for basket bottom. Basket bottom will remain unstitched.

2. Cut away the three outermost rows of holes from 4½" plastic canvas radial circle for glass holder base. Base will remain unstitched.

3. Stitch pieces following graphs, working yellow French Knots when background stitching is completed.

4. Using black through step 6, Overcast basket handle and top edges of basket sides. Whipstitch sides together, then Whipstitch sides to unstitched basket bottom. Place handle ends behind white part of candy corn on opposite sides of basket; tack handle to top edges of candy corn.

5. For glass holder Overcast top edge of side, then Whipstitch short edges together. Whipstitch bottom edge to unstitched radial circle base.

6. For napkin ring, Whipstitch short edges of ring to each side of candy corn along orange section. Overcast all remaining edges.

COLOR KEY
BASKET

Plastic Canvas Yarn	Yards
■ Black #00	24
☐ White #41	4
☐ Yellow #57	8
▨ Bright orange #58	10
○ Yellow #57 French Knot	

Color numbers given are for Uniek Needloft plastic canvas yarn.

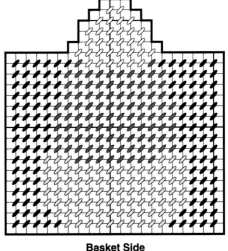

Basket Side
21 holes x 22 holes
Cut 4

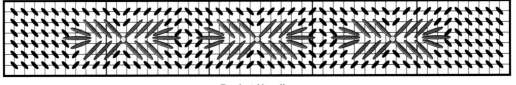

Basket Handle
49 holes x 7 holes
Cut 1

Halloween   Halloween   Halloween   Halloween   Halloween   Halloween

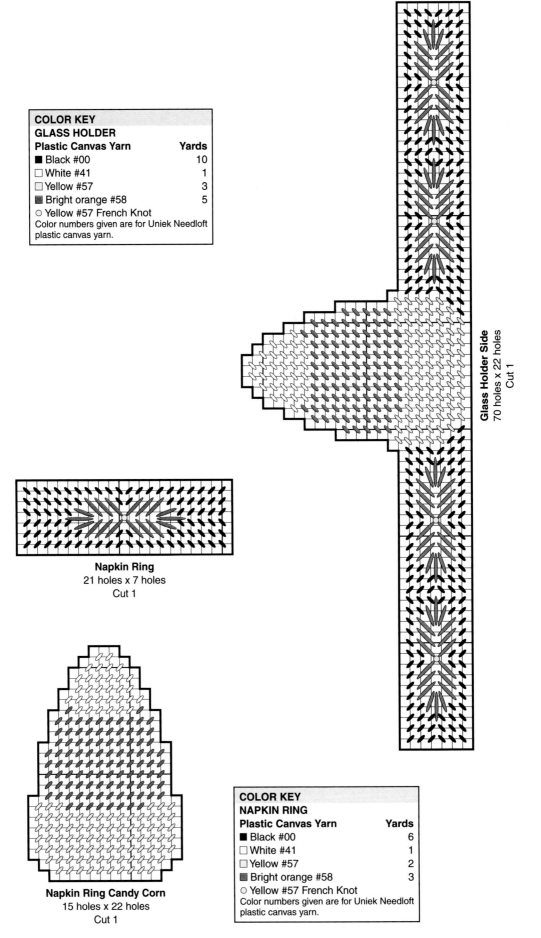

COLOR KEY
GLASS HOLDER

Plastic Canvas Yarn	Yards
■ Black #00	10
□ White #41	1
□ Yellow #57	3
▨ Bright orange #58	5
○ Yellow #57 French Knot	

Color numbers given are for Uniek Needloft plastic canvas yarn.

Glass Holder Side
70 holes x 22 holes
Cut 1

Napkin Ring
21 holes x 7 holes
Cut 1

Napkin Ring Candy Corn
15 holes x 22 holes
Cut 1

COLOR KEY
NAPKIN RING

Plastic Canvas Yarn	Yards
■ Black #00	6
□ White #41	1
□ Yellow #57	2
▨ Bright orange #58	3
○ Yellow #57 French Knot	

Color numbers given are for Uniek Needloft plastic canvas yarn.

Halloween   Halloween   Halloween   Halloween   Halloween   Halloween

FRIENDLY GHOULS
Lollipop Covers

Designs by Vicki Blizzard

Delight young trick-or-treaters with a lollipop treat covered in one of these fun covers!

Skill Level: Beginner

Finished Size

Jack-o'-Lantern: 2⅜" W x 2¾" H

Smilin' Frank: 2½" W x 3" H

Ghosty: 2½" W x 3⅛" H

Wacky Witch: 4½" W x 4½" H

Skull: 2½" W x 3¼" H

Materials

- ½ sheet Uniek Needloft 7-count plastic canvas
- Scraps of black, orange, pastel green and white 7-count plastic canvas
- Spinrite plastic canvas yarn as listed in color key
- DMC #3 pearl cotton as listed in color key
- #16 tapestry needle
- 6" ⅛"-wide green satin ribbon
- Hot-glue gun

Cutting & Stitching

1. Cut all front pieces from clear plastic canvas according to graphs.

2. Cut Jack-o'-Lantern back from orange plastic canvas, Wacky Witch and Smilin' Frank backs from pastel green plastic canvas, and Ghosty and Skull backs from white plastic canvas. Back pieces will remain unstitched.

3. Cut witch hat and hat dangle from black plastic canvas following graphs.

4. Stitch hat pieces and front pieces following graphs, working uncoded areas on Ghosty and Skull with white Continental Stitches.

5. Work Backstitches, Straight Stitches, French Knots and Couching Stitches when background stitching is completed.

talloween   Halloween   Halloween   Halloween   Halloween   Halloween

6. Overcast hat and hat dangle with black. Glue wrong side of hat dangle to right side of hat, making sure top edges are even. Tie green satin ribbon in a bow and glue to witch's hat.

Lollipop Cover Assembly

1. Overcast bottom edges of front pieces from dot to dot, then Whipstitch remaining edges of corresponding fronts and backs together following graphs.

2. For witch, attach a 3" length of purple grape yarn to sides of head where indicated on graph; tie ends in a secure knot, unravel and trim to ¾"–1".

3. Glue hat at a slight angle to head front.

Pocket Assembly (optional)

1. Overcast top edges of front pieces, then Whipstitch remaining edges of fronts and backs together following graphs.

2. Finish witch's hair following step 2 of lollipop covers. Glue hat to front of head. 🎃

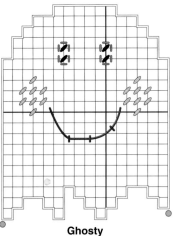

Ghosty
16 holes x 20 holes
Cut 1 from clear for front
Stitch as graphed
Cut 1 from white for back
Do not stitch

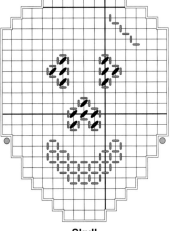

Skull
16 holes x 21 holes
Cut 1 from clear for front
Stitch as graphed
Cut 1 from white for back
Do not stitch

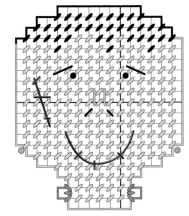

Smilin' Frank
16 holes x 19 holes
Cut 1 from clear for front
Stitch as graphed
Cut 1 from pastel green for back
Do not stitch

Wacky Witch Hat Dangle
4 holes x 5 holes
Cut 1 from black

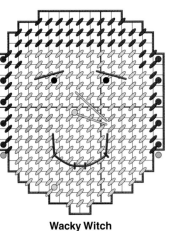

Jack-o'-Lantern
15 holes x 18 holes
Cut 1 from clear for front
Stitch as graphed
Cut 1 from orange for back
Do not stitch

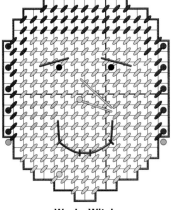

Wacky Witch
16 holes x 19 holes
Cut 1 from clear for front
Stitch as graphed
Cut 1 from pastel green for back
Do not stitch

Wacky Witch Hat
20 holes x 13 holes
Cut 1 from black

Halloween   Halloween   Halloween   Halloween   Halloween   Halloween

*Spooky bats and ghosts decorate this trio of accents that includes
a wreath, a door hanger and a wall hanging!*

Skill Level: Beginner

Finished Size
Wreath: 16⅜" W x 12" H
Door Hanger: 14¼" W x 10½" H
Wall Hanging: 6⅛" W x 19¼" H

Wreath

Materials
- 2 sheets 7-count plastic canvas
- Worsted weight yarn as listed in color key
- #16 tapestry needle
- Hot-glue gun or craft glue

Instructions
1. Cut two small bats, one large bat, one pumpkin and

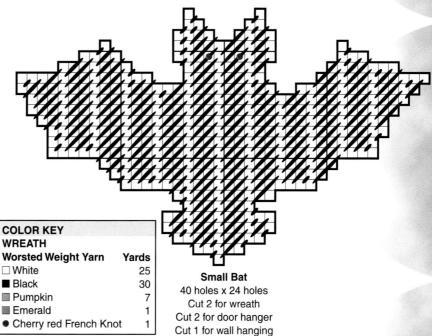

Small Bat
40 holes x 24 holes
Cut 2 for wreath
Cut 2 for door hanger
Cut 1 for wall hanging

COLOR KEY	
WREATH	
Worsted Weight Yarn	**Yards**
□ White	25
■ Black	30
▨ Pumpkin	7
▨ Emerald	1
● Cherry red French Knot	1

Halloween   Halloween   Halloween   Halloween   Halloween   Halloween

two ghosts from plastic canvas according to graphs (pages 103, 105 and 106).

2. Stitch pieces following graphs, reversing one ghost before stitching. Work cherry red French Knots for bat eyes when background stitching is completed. Overcast with adjacent colors.

3. Using photo as a guide, glue wings of small bats behind pumpkin. Glue one ghost to front of each small bat. Glue wings of large bat to bottom of ghosts.

4. Hang as desired.

Wall Hanging

Materials
- 🎃 1 sheet 7-count plastic canvas
- 🎃 Worsted weight yarn as listed in color key
- 🎃 #16 tapestry needle

Instructions
1. Cut one small bat, one pumpkin and one ghost from plastic canvas according to graphs (pages 103, 105 and 106).

2. Stitch pieces following graphs, working cherry red French Knots for bat eyes when background stitching is completed. Overcast with adjacent colors.

3. Using photo as guide, cut two 5" lengths pumpkin yarn. Attach one length yarn to bottom backside of small bat and to top backside of pumpkin. Attach remaining length to bottom backside of pumpkin and top backside of ghost.

4. Hang as desired.

Door Hanger

Materials
- 🎃 1 sheet 7-count plastic canvas

Halloween   Halloween   Halloween   Halloween   Halloween   Halloweer

- 🎃 Worsted weight yarn as listed in color key
- 🎃 #16 tapestry needle
- 🎃 Hot-glue gun or craft glue

Instructions

1. Cut two small bats, one large bat and one pumpkin from plastic canvas according to graphs (pages 103, 105 and 106).

2. Stitch pieces following graphs, working cherry red French Knots for bat eyes when background stitching is completed. Overcast with adjacent colors.

3. Using photo as guide, cut two 6" lengths black yarn. Attach one length to each small bat at bottom backside. Attach remaining ends to backside of large bat where indicated on graph. Glue wings of small bats behind pumpkin.

4. Hang as desired. 🎃

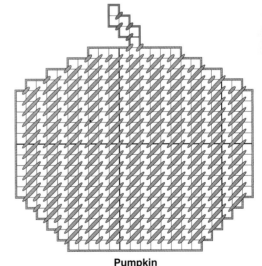

Pumpkin
23 holes x 23 holes
Cut 1 for wreath
Cut 1 for door hanger
Cut 1 for wall hanging

COLOR KEY		
DOOR HANGER		
Worsted Weight Yarn		**Yards**
■ Black		30
▨ Pumpkin		7
▨ Emerald		1
● Cherry red French Knot		1
● Attach hanging yarn		

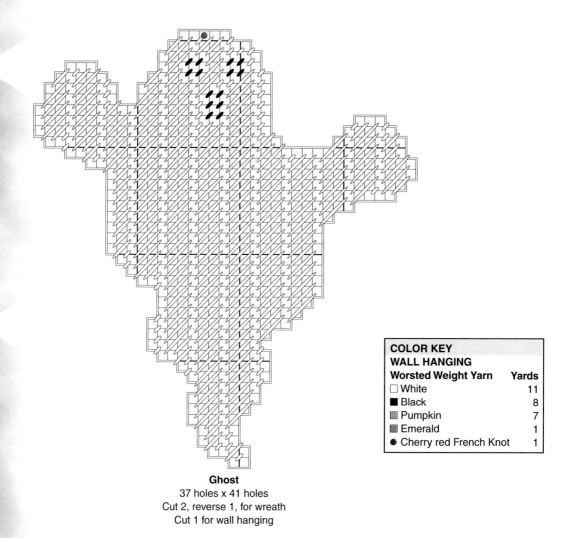

Ghost
37 holes x 41 holes
Cut 2, reverse 1, for wreath
Cut 1 for wall hanging

COLOR KEY	
WALL HANGING	
Worsted Weight Yarn	**Yards**
☐ White	11
■ Black	8
▨ Pumpkin	7
▨ Emerald	1
● Cherry red French Knot	1

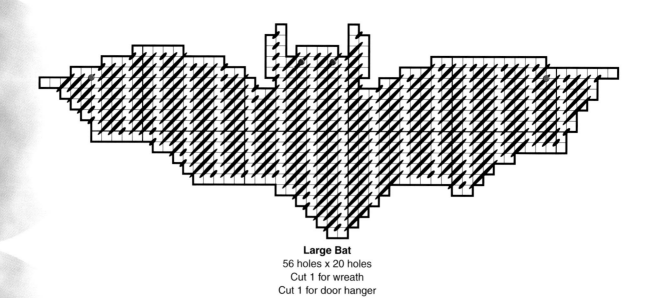

Large Bat
56 holes x 20 holes
Cut 1 for wreath
Cut 1 for door hanger

Halloween   Halloween   Halloween   Halloween   Halloween   Halloween

HALLOWEEN
Door Hangers

Designs by Kimberly A. Suber

Welcome trick-or-treaters into your home with one or both of these spooky door hangers!

Skill Level: Beginner

Finished Size

3⅛" W x 9½" H

Materials

Each Hanger

- 🎃 ¼ sheet 7-count plastic canvas
- 🎃 Worsted weight yarn as listed in color key
- 🎃 #16 tapestry needle
- 🎃 Hot-glue gun or craft glue

Instructions

1. Cut plastic canvas according to graphs.

2. Stitch pieces following graphs, working uncoded areas on witch hanger with orange Continental Stitches and uncoded areas on ghost and pumpkin hanger with purple Continental Stitches.

3. Backstitch mouths and ghost's nose and work all French Knots with 4 plies black yarn. Backstitch outlines and letters on witch's pot with 2 plies yarn.

4. Overcast witch hanger with orange. Overcast ghost and pumpkin hanger with purple.

5. Cut one 6" length each of yellow and fuchsia yarn. Tie each in a bow. Glue yellow bow to ghost and pumpkin hanger; glue fuchsia bow to witch hanger. 🎃

COLOR KEY

GHOST & PUMPKIN HANGER

Worsted Weight Yarn	Yards
□ White	8
■ Black	5
▨ Orange	2
▨ Bright green	1
▨ Green	1
■ Fuchsia	1
Uncoded areas are purple Continental Stitches	15
╱ Purple Overcasting	
╱ Black Backstitch and Straight Stitch	
● Black French Knot	

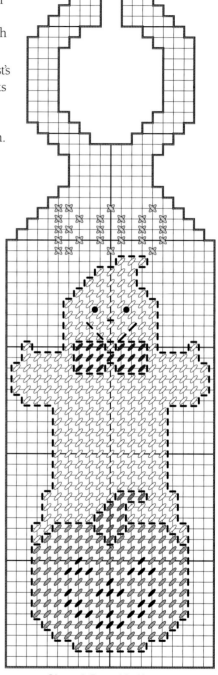

Ghost & Pumpkin Hanger
20 holes x 63 holes
Cut 1

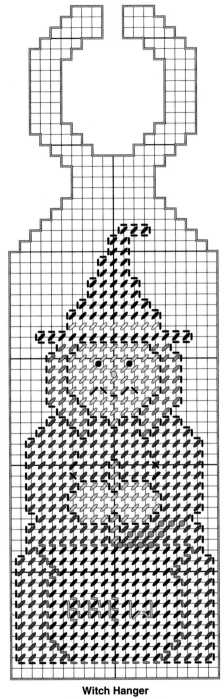

Witch Hanger
20 holes x 63 holes
Cut 1

COLOR KEY	
WITCH HANGER	
Worsted Weight Yarn	**Yards**
■ Black	10
■ Purple	4
▢ Bright green	2
▨ Gray	2
▢ Yellow	1
▨ Tan	1
Uncoded areas are orange	
Continental Stitches	12
⁄ Orange Overcasting	
⁄ Black Backstitch	
⁄ Bright green Backstitch	
⁄ Gray Backstitch	
● Black French Knot	
○ Bright green French Knot	
◉ Gray French Knot	

JACK-O'-LANTERN
Hearts

Designs by Angie Arickx

Hang this fun Halloween decoration on a door, or back it with magnets to stick on your fridge! A fun third option is to use each motif as a coaster!

Skill Level: Beginner

Finished Size
Door Decoration:
3½" W x 10⅛" H
Coaster: 3½" W x 3½" H

Materials
- ½ sheet 7-count plastic canvas
- Uniek Needloft plastic canvas yarn as listed in color key
- #16 tapestry needle

Instructions
1. Cut plastic canvas according to graphs (page 111).
2. Stitch and Overcast pieces following graphs, working Backstitches on door decoration while Overcasting.
3. Hang decoration as desired.

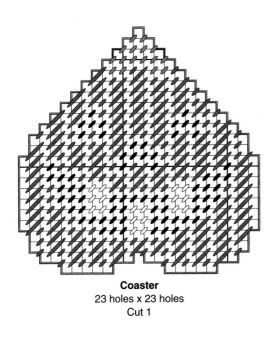

Coaster
23 holes x 23 holes
Cut 1

COLOR KEY

Plastic Canvas Yarn	Yards
■ Black #00	6
▨ Holly #27	2
☐ White #41	1
▤ Bittersweet #52	23
╱ Holly #27 Straight Stitch	
╱ Bittersweet #52 Backstitch	

Color numbers given are for Uniek Needloft plastic canvas yarn.

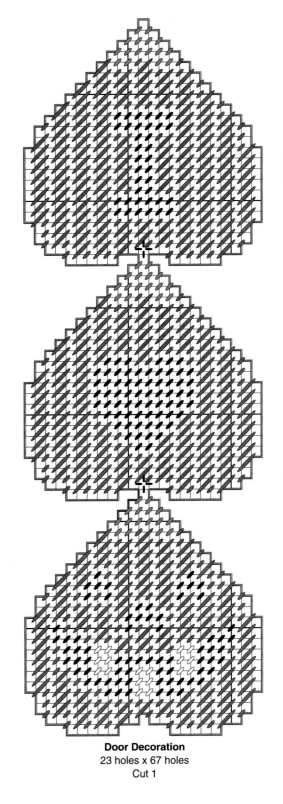

Door Decoration
23 holes x 67 holes
Cut 1

Halloween   Halloween   Halloween   Halloween   Halloween   Halloween

HARVESTTIME
Wall Decor

Design by Terry A. Ricioli

Perfect for hanging throughout the fall season, this colorful project is an attractive display of autumn beauty.

Skill Level: Beginner

Finished Size

Approximately 18" W x 9" H

Materials

* 1½ sheets 7-count plastic canvas
* Uniek Needloft plastic canvas yarn as listed in color key
* #16 tapestry needle
* Hot-glue gun

Instructions

1. Cut plastic canvas according to graphs (below and page 114). Hanger will remain unstitched.

2. Stitch pieces following graphs, working rust Continental Stitches on pumpkin first, then filling in with tangerine Slanting Gobelin Stitches. Work pumpkin Straight Stitches on oak leaves when background stitching is completed.

3. Overcast pieces following graphs.

4. Using photo as a guide, arrange pieces as desired, then glue in place. Glue hanger just under pumpkin stem on backside. ✿

COLOR KEY	
Plastic Canvas Yarn	**Yards**
■ Red #01	5
▨ Burgundy #03	1
▢ Rust #09	14
☐ Tangerine #11	12
▨ Pumpkin #12	30
■ Maple #13	3
■ Cinnamon #14	1
☐ Straw #19	8
▨ Christmas green #28	4
■ Purple #46	4
Uncoded areas are plum #59 Continental Stitches	8
✎ Plum #58 Overcasting	
✎ Sundown #10 Overcasting	4
✎ Pumpkin #12 Straight Stitch	
Color numbers given are for Uniek Needloft plastic canvas yarn.	

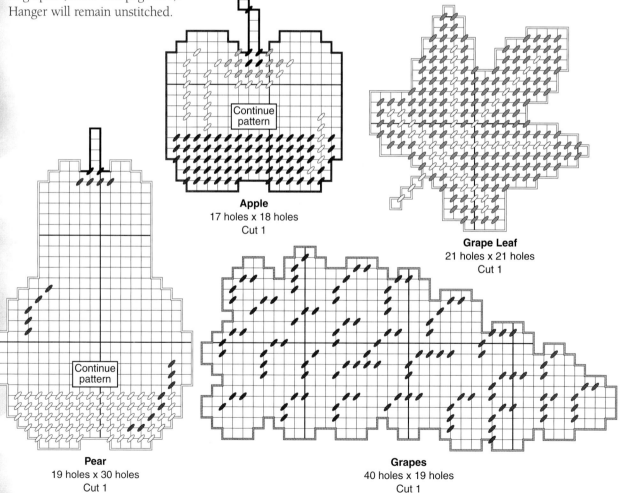

Apple
17 holes x 18 holes
Cut 1

Grape Leaf
21 holes x 21 holes
Cut 1

Pear
19 holes x 30 holes
Cut 1

Grapes
40 holes x 19 holes
Cut 1

Thanksgiving Thanksgiving Thanksgiving Thanksgiving Thanksgiving

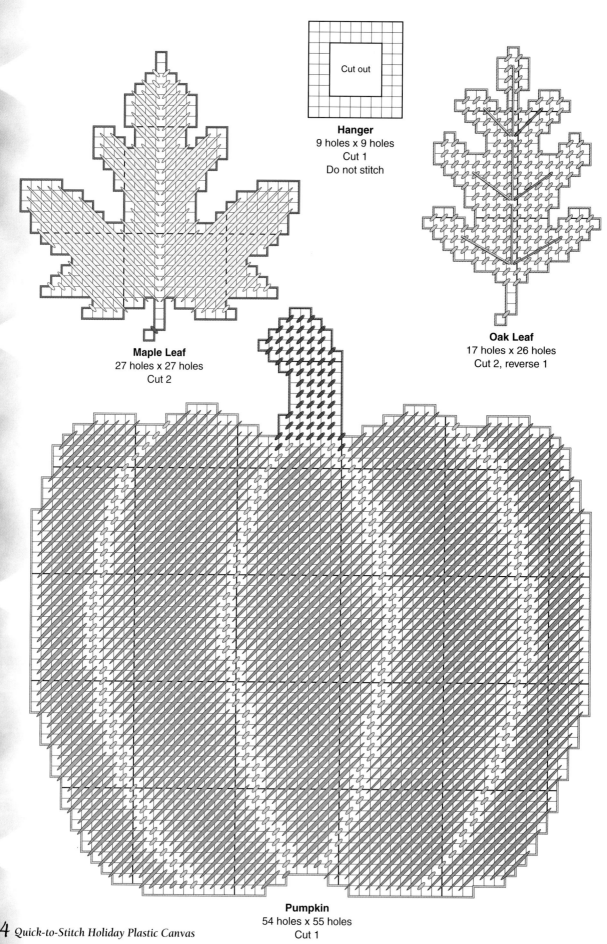

Hanger
9 holes x 9 holes
Cut 1
Do not stitch

Cut out

Maple Leaf
27 holes x 27 holes
Cut 2

Oak Leaf
17 holes x 26 holes
Cut 2, reverse 1

Pumpkin
54 holes x 55 holes
Cut 1

Thanksgiving   Thanksgiving   Thanksgiving   Thanksgiving   Thanksgiving

WHIMSICAL
Turkey Magnet

Design by Vicki Blizzard

Give your family a good chuckle with this hilarious Thanksgiving magnet featuring Tom the turkey encouraging all to eat veggies!

Skill Level: Beginner

Finished Size

7⅝" W x 5½" H

Materials

- ½ sheet Uniek Quick-Count 7-count plastic canvas
- Uniek Needloft plastic canvas yarn as listed in color key
- DMC #3 pearl cotton as listed in color key
- Kreinik Heavy (#32) Braid as listed in color key
- #16 tapestry needle
- 2 (4mm) round black cabochons from The Beadery
- Wooden craft pick or large toothpick.
- 12" ½"-wide magnet strip
- Jewel glue
- Hot-glue gun

Instructions

1. Cut plastic canvas according to graphs (page 116).

2. Stitch and Overcast corn and broccoli following graphs, working background on ear of corn with yellow Continental Stitches and background on broccoli with holly Continental Stitches. Work French Knots on top of background stitching.

3. With gold, Overcast feet, then work Straight Stitches. Stitch and Overcast remaining pieces following graphs, reversing one wing before stitching and working uncoded backgrounds on sign and base with white Continental Stitches.

4. When background stitching

and Overcasting are completed, work Backstitches and Straight Stitches on base, sign and head. Cut a short length of holly yarn, thread through top right hole of carrot. Tie in a knot, trim to desired length and fray edges.

5. Using photo as a guide throughout assembly and using hot-glue gun through step 7, glue feet to base along bottom edge. Center and glue head to tail feathers.

6. Glue wooden craft pick to back of sign for handle. Place one wing on each side of base. Glue wooden handle behind one wing and veggies behind other wing, then glue wings to base, handle and veggies.

7. Cut magnet strip into three equal pieces. Glue magnets to backside, placing one magnet behind tail feathers and one on each side.

8. Glue cabochons to turkey head for eyes, using jewel glue. 🐦

COLOR KEY	
Plastic Canvas Yarn	**Yards**
■ Black #00	1
■ Red #01	8
■ Maple #13	3
▨ Gold #17	4
■ Holly #27	3
▨ Camel #43	5
■ Bittersweet #52	3
□ Yellow #57	2
Uncoded areas are white #41	
Continental Stitches	12
╱ Red #01 Straight Stitch	
╱ Maple #13 Straight Stitch	
╱ Gold #17 Straight Stitch	
● Holly #27 French Knot	
○ Yellow #57 French Knot	
#3 Pearl Cotton	
╱ Black #310 Backstitch	2
Heavy (#32) Braid	
╱ Gold #00HL Straight Stitch	½
Color numbers given are for Uniek Needloft plastic canvas yarn, DMC #3 pearl cotton and Kreinik Heavy (#32) Braid.	

Thanksgiving   Thanksgiving   Thanksgiving   Thanksgiving   Thanksgiving

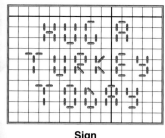

Sign
15 holes x 11 holes
Cut 1

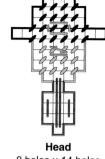

Head
9 holes x 14 holes
Cut 1

COLOR KEY

Plastic Canvas Yarn	Yards
■ Black #00	1
■ Red #01	8
■ Maple #13	3
■ Gold #17	4
■ Holly #27	3
▨ Camel #43	5
■ Bittersweet #52	3
□ Yellow #57	2
Uncoded areas are white #41	
Continental Stitches	12
╱ Red #01 Straight Stitch	
╱ Maple #13 Straight Stitch	
╱ Gold #17 Straight Stitch	
● Holly #27 French Knot	
○ Yellow #57 French Knot	
#3 Pearl Cotton	
╱ Black #310 Backstitch	2
Heavy (#32) Braid	
╱ Gold #00HL Straight Stitch	½

Color numbers given are for Uniek Needloft plastic canvas yarn, DMC #3 pearl cotton and Kreinik Heavy (#32) Braid.

Broccoli
6 holes x 9 holes
Cut 1

Foot
5 holes x 4 holes
Cut 2

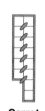

Corn
8 holes x 10 holes
Cut 1

Carrot
2 holes x 8 holes
Cut 1

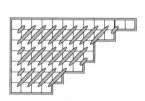

Wing
12 holes x 7 holes
Cut 2, reverse 1

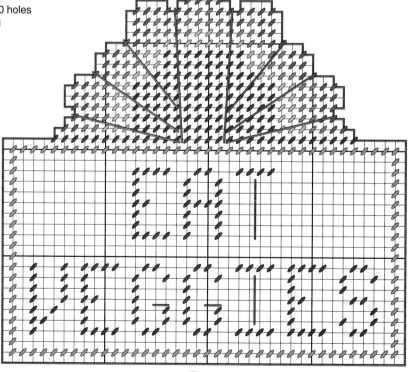

Base
39 holes x 35 holes
Cut 1

116 Quick-to-Stitch Holiday Plastic Canvas

Thanksgiving *Thanksgiving* *Thanksgiving* *Thanksgiving* *Thanksgiving*

AUTUMN TABLE
Accessories

Designs by Carol Krob

Stitched with sparkling metallic ribbon, this set of napkin rings, goblet decorations and place cards will add to your Thanksgiving dinner table! Photo on page 118.

Skill Level: Beginner

Finished Size

Napkin Ring: 2½" W x 2½" H x 1½" in diameter

Place Card: 4½" W x1⅞" H

Goblet Decoration: 2½" W x 1" H

Materials

- ⅔ sheet tan 10-count plastic canvas
- ½ sheet ivory 10-count plastic canvas
- DMC #3 pearl cotton as listed in color key
- Kreinik ⅛" Ribbon as listed in color key
- Small amount gold #002HL Kreinik Very Fine (#4) Braid
- #20 tapestry needle
- #24 tapestry needle
- Heavy paper in coordinating color
- Calligraphy marker with 2mm tip in desired color
- 18" ¼"-wide decorative braid in coordinating colors

Napkin Rings

1. Cut two leaf motifs and two napkin rings from tan plastic canvas according to graphs (below and page 119).

2. Using #20 tapestry needle, stitch rings and one leaf follow-ing graphs. Stitch remaining leaf reversing vintage red and vintage sienna.

3. Using vintage gold through-out, Overcast leaves and top and bottom edges of rings. Whipstitch short edges of rings together.

4. Using gold very fine (#4) braid and #24 tapestry needle, attach center backside of one leaf to each ring at seam.

Goblet Decorations

1. Cut two goblet decorations from tan plastic canvas according to graph (page 118).

2. Using #20 tapestry needle, stitch one piece following graph and one replacing vintage sienna with vintage red. Overcast with vintage gold.

3. Cut ¼"-wide decorative braid in half. Using gold very fine (#4) braid and #24 tapestry needle, attach one length of braid to cen-ter backside of each goblet deco-ration. Tie braid around stem of goblet, trimming ends as desired.

Place Cards

1. From ivory plastic canvas, cut two place card front pieces according to graph (page 119); cut two 44-hole x 18-hole pieces for place card front liners. Liners will remain unstitched.

2. From tan plastic canvas, cut two 44-hole x 18-hole pieces for place card backs. Backs will remain unstitched.

3. Using #20 tapestry needle, stitch one front as graphed and one reversing vintage red and vintage sienna.

4. Using vintage gold through step 5, for each place card, Overcast inside edges and side edges on front.

5. Place front liner behind front piece and Whipstitch bottom edges together. Place back piece behind liner, then Whipstitch top edges of back, front and front liner together through all three thicknesses.

6. For each place card, cut a 4¼" x 1½" piece from heavy paper. Center and print desired name on paper with calligraphy mark-er. Insert paper between front piece and front liner so that name is centered in opening.

COLOR KEY
NAPKIN RINGS

⅛" Ribbon	Yards
☐ Vintage gold #002V	4
■ Vintage red #003V	3
▨ Vintage sienna #152V	3
■ Vintage verdigris #154V	4

Color numbers given are for Kreinik ⅛" Ribbon.

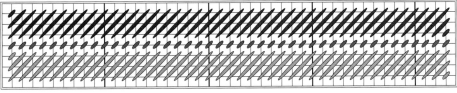

Napkin Ring
44 holes x 8 holes
Cut 2 from tan

Thanksgiving Thanksgiving Thanksgiving Thanksgiving Thanksgiving

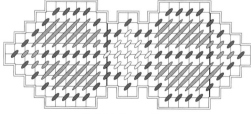

Goblet Decoration
24 holes x 10 holes
Cut 2 from tan
Stitch 1 as graphed
Stitch 1 replacing vintage
sienna with vintage red

COLOR KEY	
GOBLET DECORATIONS	
⅛" Ribbon	**Yards**
☐ Vintage gold #002V	2
■ Vintage red #003V	2
▨ Vintage sienna #152V	2
■ Vintage verdigris #154V	2
Color numbers given are for Kreinik ⅛" Ribbon.	

Thanksgiving Thanksgiving Thanksgiving Thanksgiving Thanksgiving

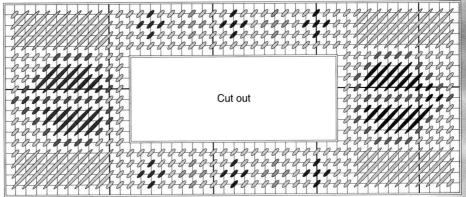

Place Card Front
44 holes x 18 holes
Cut 2 from ivory
Stitch 1 as graphed
Stitch 1 reversing
vintage red and vintage sienna

COLOR KEY
PLACE CARDS

#3 Pearl Cotton	Yards
☐ Ultra very light beige brown #543	
⅛" Ribbon	4
■ Vintage red #003V	
■ Vintage sienna #152V	2
■ Vintage verdigris #154V	3
⟋ Vintage gold #002V Overcasting	3
and Whipstitching	2

Color numbers given are for DMC #3 pearl cotton
and Kreinik ⅛" Ribbon.

Napkin Ring Leaves
24 holes x 24 holes
Cut 2 from tan
Stitch 1 as graphed
Stitch 1 reversing
vintage red and vintage sienna

COLOR KEY
NAPKIN RINGS

⅛" Ribbon	Yards
☐ Vintage gold #002V	4
■ Vintage red #003V	3
☐ Vintage sienna #152V	3
■ Vintage verdigris #154V	4

Color numbers given are for Kreinik
⅛" Ribbon.

Thanksgiving   Thanksgiving   Thanksgiving   Thanksgiving   Thanksgiving

LITTLE PILGRIMS
Basket

Design by Janelle Giese

Charm your Thanksgiving dinner guests with this delightful, decorative basket!

Skill Level: Beginner

Finished Size

Man: 2½" W x 4¼" H

Lady: 2¾" W x 4⅛" H

Materials

- ½ sheet 7-count plastic canvas
- Uniek Needloft plastic canvas yarn as listed in color key
- Kreinik ⅛" Ribbon as listed in color key
- DMC #5 pearl cotton as listed in color key
- #16 tapestry needle
- Harvest red #R69 Classic Gingham Paper Twist by Maxwell Wellington
- Small amount raffia straw
- Purchased basket with handle (sample basket is approximately 6" x 8" in diameter x 5¼" D)
- Carpet thread
- Thick white glue

Instructions

1. Cut plastic canvas according to graphs.

2. Stitch and Overcast pieces following graphs. When background stitching and Overcasting are completed, work Backstitches and Straight Stitches, working four stitches for each eye.

3. For bow, cut a 6" length of ⅛"-wide gold ribbon. Thread ends from back to front through holes indicated with blue dots on lady pilgrim; tie a small bow and trim ends.

4. Using photo as a guide through step 7, tie gingham twisted paper ribbon in a bow with long tails, making bow about the size of one basket side. Tie raffia straw in a bow slightly smaller than gingham bow.

5. Center raffia straw bow on gingham bow, then attach center of bows to basket with carpet thread, knotting off thread inside basket.

6. Place pilgrims side by side on front of bow, then attach with carpet thread by going through pilgrims, bow and basket, knotting off thread inside basket.

7. Glue tails of gingham bow to basket sides at base of handle; cut ends in a "V." ❧

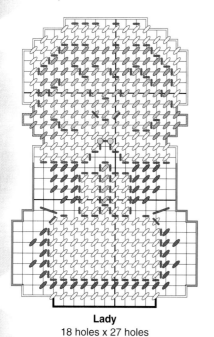

Lady
18 holes x 27 holes
Cut 1

COLOR KEY

Plastic Canvas Yarn	Yards
■ Black #00	2
▨ Rust #09	1
■ Cinnamon #14	2
☐ Eggshell #39	5
▨ Camel #43	2
▨ Flesh tone #56	3
Uncoded areas are brown #15 Continental Stitches	4
╱ Brown #15 Overcasting	
⅛" Ribbon	
╱ Gold #002HL Backstitch	1
#5 Pearl Cotton	
╱ Black #310 Backstitch and Straight Stitch	5

Color numbers given are for Uniek Needloft plastic canvas yarn, Kreinik ⅛" Ribbon and DMC #5 pearl cotton.

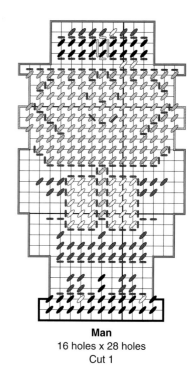

Man
16 holes x 28 holes
Cut 1

Thanksgiving   Thanksgiving   Thanksgiving   Thanksgiving   Thanksgiving

TURKEY
Napkin Holder

Design by Robin Petrina

Here's a decorative, yet very practical, project you can use
on your dining table—an attractive napkin holder!

Skill Level: Beginner

Finished Size

11⅝" W x 7⅞" H x 1⅜" D

Materials

- 1 sheet clear 7-count plastic canvas
- ⅔ sheet brown 7-count plastic canvas
- Worsted weight yarn as listed in color key
- #16 tapestry needle
- 2 (7mm) movable eyes
- Small amount floral clay
- Plastic wrap
- Hot-glue gun

Instructions

1. Cut four leaf fronts, one turkey front, one turkey back and all base pieces from clear plastic canvas; cut four leaf backs from brown plastic canvas according to graphs. Leaf backs will remain unstitched.

2. Stitch clear plastic canvas pieces following graphs, working

one leaf with burgundy as graphed, one with pumpkin, one with honey gold and one with rust. Work Straight Stitches on leaves when background stitching is completed.

3. Place one unstitched leaf back behind each stitched leaf front, matching edges; Whipstitch each front and back together with adjacent colors. Overcast beak with honey gold.

Turkey Beak
3 holes x 3 holes
Cut 1 from clear

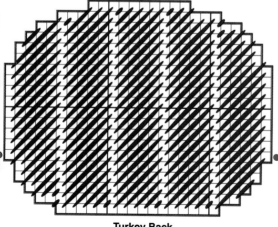

Turkey Back
26 holes x 20 holes
Cut 1 from clear

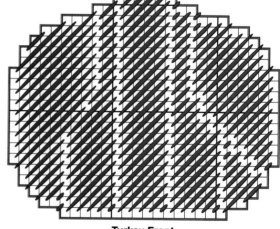

Turkey Front
26 holes x 36 holes
Cut 1 from clear

Thanksgiving   Thanksgiving   Thanksgiving   Thanksgiving   Thanksgiving

4. Using brown throughout, Overcast turkey front and back. Whipstitch base short sides to base long sides, then Whipstitch base bottom to sides. Shape floral clay to fit inside base, then wrap in plastic wrap and place in base. Whipstitch top to sides.

5. Using photo as a guide throughout assembly, glue right side of leaves to right side of turkey back around top and sides from dot to dot, overlapping leaves as necessary to fit.

6. Center and glue turkey front to one long side of base, making sure bottom edges are even. Repeat, gluing turkey back to remaining long side of base.

COLOR KEY	
Worsted Weight Yarn	**Yards**
■ Brown	18
■ Burgundy	9
☐ Honey gold	9
Pumpkin	9
Rust	9
✐ Burgundy Straight Stitch	

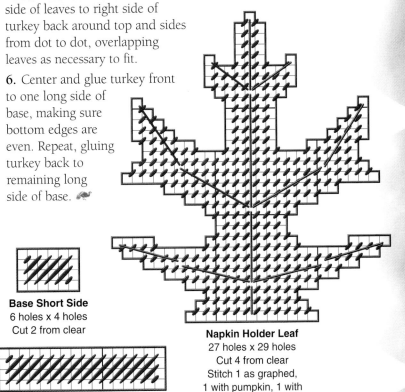

Napkin Holder Leaf
27 holes x 29 holes
Cut 4 from clear
Stitch 1 as graphed,
1 with pumpkin, 1 with
honey gold and 1 with rust
Cut 4 from brown
Do not stitch

Base Short Side
6 holes x 4 holes
Cut 2 from clear

Base Top & Bottom
16 holes x 6 holes
Cut 2 from clear

Base Long Side
16 holes x 4 holes
Cut 2 from clear

Thanksgiving   Thanksgiving   Thanksgiving   Thanksgiving   Thanksgiving

PILGRIM & INDIAN
Wall Decor

Design by Celia Lange Designs

This decorative wall picture will inspire you to celebrate
Thanksgiving with thanks and joy.

Thanksgiving   Thanksgiving   Thanksgiving   Thanksgiving   Thanksgiving

Skill Level: Beginner

Finished Size

9½" W x 8⅝" H

Materials

- 🦃 1 sheet Darice Ultra Stiff 7-count plastic canvas
- 🦃 Coats & Clark Red Heart Classic worsted weight yarn Art. E267 as listed in color key
- 🦃 Coats & Clark Red Heart Super Saver worsted weight yarn Art. E301 as listed in color key
- 🦃 DMC #3 pearl cotton as listed in color key
- 🦃 Kreinik ⅛" Ribbon as listed in color key
- 🦃 #16 tapestry needle
- 🦃 Assorted vegetable buttons
- 🦃 Hot-glue gun

Instructions

1. Cut plastic canvas according to graphs (below and page 126).

2. Stitch and Overcast sign following graph, working uncoded area with eggshell Continental Stitches. Embroider words with black #3 pearl cotton.

3. Stitch and Overcast Indian and pilgrim pieces following graphs, reversing one hand before stitching.

4. Embroider faces, hands and clothing detail on pilgrim tops with black pearl cotton. Embroider shoes and hat with ⅛"-wide silver ribbon.

5. Embroider Indian brave's lacing with coffee and Indian maiden's lacing with mid brown. Wrap Indian maiden's hair with one strand warm brown, securing on backside.

6. Following photo throughout, glue Indian and pilgrim pieces to backside of sign in order shown. Clip off backs of buttons and glue to sign. Glue one hand to each side of sign. 🦃

COLOR KEY

Worsted Weight Yarn	Yards
☐ White #1	4
■ Black #12	10
■ Bronze #286	2
☐ Gold #321	2
▨ Tan #334	8
▨ Warm brown #336	6
■ Coffee #365	3
▨ Nickel #401	1
☐ Silver #412	8
Uncoded area on sign is eggshell #111 Continental Stitches	20
Uncoded areas on Indian maiden are warm brown #336 Continental Stitches	
Uncoded areas on Indian man are mid brown #339 Continental Stitches	4
⁄ Eggshell #111 Overcasting	
⁄ Mid brown #339 Backstitch, Straight Stitch and Overcasting	
⁄ Warm brown #336 Straight Stitch	
⁄ Coffee #365 Straight Stitch	
⊙ Mid brown #339 French Knot	
⅛" Ribbon	
■ Silver #001	1
#3 Pearl Cotton	
⁄ Black #310 Backstitch and Straight Stitch	7
⊙ Black #310 French Knot	

Color numbers given are for Red Heart Classic worsted weight yarn Art. E267, Red Heart Super Saver worsted weight yarn Art. E301, Kreinik ⅛" Ribbon and DMC #3 pearl cotton.

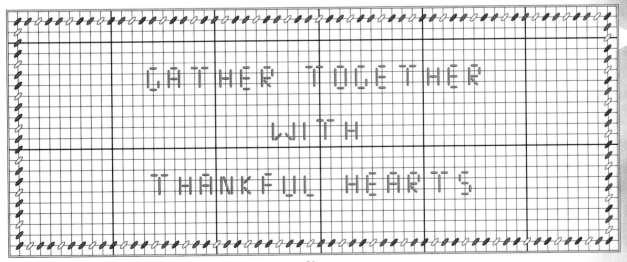

Sign
59 holes x 23 holes
Cut 1

Thanksgiving   Thanksgiving   Thanksgiving   Thanksgiving   Thanksgiving

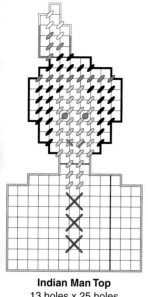

Indian Man Top
13 holes x 25 holes
Cut 1

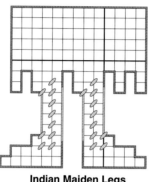

Indian Maiden Top
13 holes x 20 holes
Cut 1

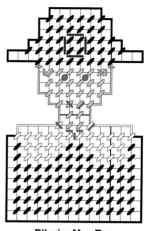

Pilgrim Man Top
13 holes x 20 holes
Cut 1

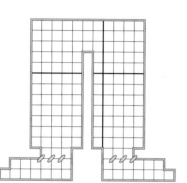

Indian Maiden Legs
14 holes x 15 holes
Cut 1

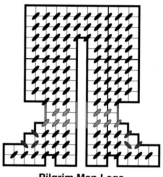

Pilgrim Man Legs
15 holes x 15 holes
Cut 1

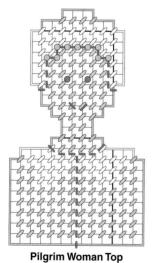

Indian Man Legs
17 holes x 15 holes
Cut 1

Hand
3 holes x 4 holes
Cut 2, reverse 1

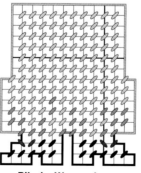

Pilgrim Woman Top
13 holes x 22 holes
Cut 1

Pilgrim Woman Legs
13 holes x 15 holes
Cut 1

COLOR KEY	
Worsted Weight Yarn	**Yards**
☐ White #1	4
■ Black #12	10
■ Bronze #286	2
☐ Gold #321	2
☐ Tan #334	8
▨ Warm brown #336	6
■ Coffee #365	3
▨ Nickel #401	1
☐ Silver #412	8
Uncoded area on sign is eggshell #111 Continental Stitches	20
Uncoded areas on Indian maiden are warm brown #336 Continental Stitches	
Uncoded areas on Indian man are mid brown #339 Continental Stitches	4
╱ Eggshell #111 Overcasting	
╱ Mid brown #339 Backstitch, Straight Stitch and Overcasting	
╱ Warm brown #336 Straight Stitch	
╱ Coffee #365 Straight Stitch	
● Mid brown #339 French Knot	
⅛" Ribbon	
■ Silver #001	1
#3 Pearl Cotton	
╱ Black #310 Backstitch and Straight Stitch	7
● Black #310 French Knot	
Color numbers given are for Red Heart Classic worsted weight yarn Art. E267, Red Heart Super Saver worsted weight yarn Art. E301, Kreinik ⅛" Ribbon and DMC #3 pearl cotton.	

Thanksgiving   Thanksgiving   Thanksgiving   Thanksgiving   Thanksgiving

AUTUMN LEAVES
Napkin Rings

Designs by Mary T. Cosgrove

Stitch a handsome napkin ring for each of your Thanksgiving dinner guests.

Skill Level: Beginner

Finished Size

Maple Leaf: 2⅛" W x 1⅝" H x 1½" in diameter

Oak Leaf: 2⅜" W x 1⅜" H x 1½" in diameter

Materials

- ½ sheet Uniek Quick-Count 7-count plastic canvas
- Uniek Needloft plastic canvas yarn as listed in color key
- #16 tapestry needle

Instructions

1. Cut plastic canvas according to graphs.

2. Stitch and Overcast leaves following graphs; working brown Straight Stitches while Overcasting stems on leaves.

3. Overlap four holes on one napkin ring forming a circle, then Overcast with brown. Repeat with remaining napkin rings.

4. For each ring, place overlapped edges of ring vertically behind leaf so leaf hides ring. Using brown yarn, attach ring to yarn on backside of leaf, going over ring several times. 🦃

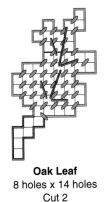

Oak Leaf
8 holes x 14 holes
Cut 2

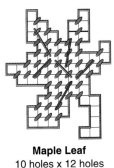

Maple Leaf
10 holes x 12 holes
Cut 2

COLOR KEY	
Plastic Canvas Yarn	**Yards**
▨ Pumpkin #12	3
▨ Gold #17	2
╱ Brown #15 Straight Stitch and Overcasting	6
Color numbers given are for Uniek Needloft plastic canvas yarn.	

Overlap   **Napkin Ring**
35 holes x 1 holes
Cut 4   Overlap

Thanksgiving   Thanksgiving   Thanksgiving   Thanksgiving   Thanksgiving

HANUKKAH BEAR
Candy Dish

Design by Celia Lange Designs

*Delight the younger members of your family
with this adorable Jewish teddy bear candy dish.*

Skill Level: Beginner

Finished Size

5⅜" W x 6¼" H x 2½" D

Materials

✡ 1 sheet Darice Ultra Stiff 7-count plastic canvas

✡ Small amount regular 7-count plastic canvas

✡ Coats & Clark Red Heart Classic worsted weight yarn Art. E267 as listed in color key

✡ Lion Chenille acrylic yarn from Lion Brand Yarn Co. as listed in color key

✡ DMC #3 pearl cotton as listed in color key

✡ Darice metallic cord as listed in color key

✡ #16 tapestry needle

✡ Small amount medium blue felt

✡ ¾" silvertone Star of David charm

✡ 6" length silvertone chain

✡ 2 silvertone jump rings

✡ ½ yard ½"-wide silver trim

✡ 2 (18mm) brown oval movable eyes

✡ Needle-nose pliers

✡ Hot-glue gun

Instructions

1. Cut arms from regular plastic canvas; cut remaining pieces from stiff plastic canvas according to graphs (below and page 130). Cut one 25-hole x 13-hole piece from stiff plastic canvas for candy dish bottom.

2. Cut one 1" x 10" strip medium blue felt for prayer shawl. Using pattern given, cut one yarmulke from medium blue felt.

3. Stitch pieces following graphs, reversing one arm before stitching. Work white/silver metallic cord Straight Stitches on candy dish pieces when background stitching is completed. Continental Stitch candy dish bottom with true blue yarn.

4. Using white/silver metallic cord throughout, Overcast top edges of candy dish sides. Whipstitch sides together, then Whipstitch sides to bottom.

5. Using russet chenille yarn throughout, Overcast muzzle. Whipstitch top edges on arms to straight edges just below shoulders on bear body. Overcast remaining edges. Work black pearl cotton embroidery on muzzle.

6. Cut two 10" strips of ½"-wide silver trim; glue trim along both long edges of prayer shawl. Glue remaining trim around outer edge of yarmulke.

7. Using photo as a guide through step 9, cut chain to fit around bear's neck; using needlenose pliers, secure ends on backside of bear with one jump ring. Attach remaining jump ring to charm and to chain so charm hangs on bear front.

8. Glue muzzle and eyes to head front. Glue prayer shawl around bear's neck and down front of bear. Glue yarmulke over top edge of bear's head between ears.

9. Glue back of candy dish to body front. Wrap arms loosely around dish, then glue paws to candy dish front. ✡

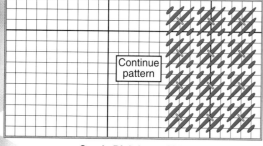

Candy Dish Long Side
25 holes x 13 holes
Cut 2 from stiff

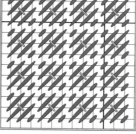

Candy Dish Short Side
13 holes x 13 holes
Cut 2 from stiff

COLOR KEY

	Yards
Worsted Weight Yarn	
■ True blue #822	12
Chenille Acrylic Yarn	
■ Russet #136	32
Metallic Cord	
⁄ White/silver #34021-112 Straight Stitch and Overcasting	9
#3 Pearl Cotton	
⁄ Black #310 Straight Stitch	1

Color numbers given are for Red Heart Classic worsted weight yarn Art. E267, Lion Brand Chenille acrylic yarn, Darice metallic cord and DMC #3 pearl cotton.

Hanukkah   Hanukkah   Hanukkah   Hanukkah   Hanukkah   Hanukkah

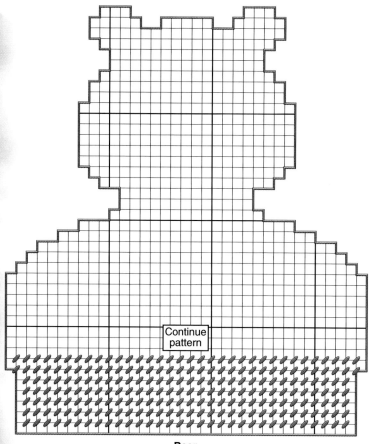

Bear
35 holes x 40 holes
Cut 1 from stiff

Continue pattern

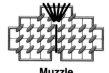

Arm
16 holes x 20 holes
Cut 2, reverse 1, from regular

Muzzle
9 holes x 5 holes
Cut 1 from stiff

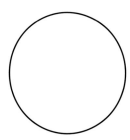

Yarmulke
Cut 1 from
medium blue felt

COLOR KEY

Worsted Weight Yarn	Yards
■ True blue #822	12
Chenille Acrylic Yarn	
■ Russet #136	32
Metallic Cord	
⁄ White/silver #34021-112	
Straight Stitch and Overcasting	9
#3 Pearl Cotton	
⁄ Black #310 Straight Stitch	1

Color numbers given are for Red Heart Classic worsted weight yarn Art. E267, Lion Brand Chenille acrylic yarn, Darice metallic cord and DMC #3 pearl cotton.

Hanukkah   Hanukkah   Hanukkah   Hanukkah   Hanukkah   Hanukkah

GOLDEN
Pendant

Design by Angie Arickx

This *quick-to-stitch* Star of David makes a meaningful wardrobe accessory when threaded onto a gold chain.

Skill Level: Beginner

Finished Size

2½" W x 2¼" H excluding chain

Materials

✡ 5" plastic canvas hexagon by Uniek

✡ ⅛"-wide Plastic Canvas 7 Metallic Needlepoint Yarn by Rainbow Gallery as listed in color key

✡ #18 tapestry needle

✡ 18" gold necklace chain

Instructions

1. Cut plastic canvas according to graph, cutting away gray areas.

2. Stitch and Overcast pendant following graph.

3. Thread gold necklace chain from front to back through holes indicated on graph with blue dots. ✡

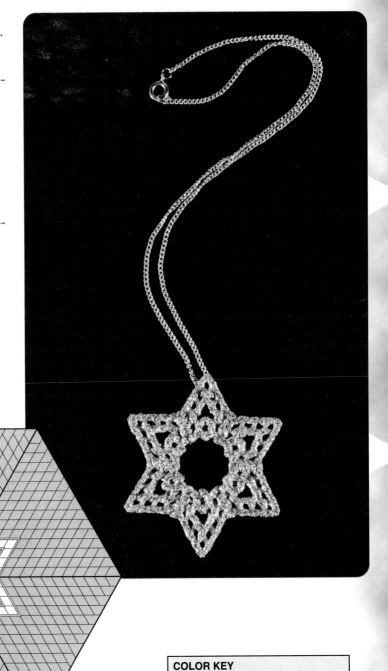

Golden Pendant
Cut 1
Cut away gray areas

Hanukkah   Hanukkah   Hanukkah   Hanukkah   Hanukkah   Hanukkah

TOUCH OF GOLD
Hanukkah Accents

Design by Vicki Blizzard

Hanukkah   Hanukkah   Hanukkah   Hanukkah   Hanukkah   Hanukkah

Whether you use these attractive accents as magnets, basket decorations or window ornaments, you'll enjoy stitching and displaying all three.

Skill Level: Beginner

Finished Size

Happy Hanukkah: 4⅝" W x 1¾" H

Menorah: 3" W x 2¾" H

Star of David: 3¾" W x 3¾" H

Materials

✡ ½ sheet Uniek Quick-Count 10-count plastic canvas

✡ DMC #3 pearl cotton as listed in color key

✡ DMC 6-strand embroidery floss as listed in color key

✡ Kreinik Heavy (#32) Braid as listed in color key

✡ Kreinik Medium (#16) Braid as listed in color key

✡ #22 tapestry needle

✡ ½"-wide self-adhesive magnet strip (optional)

✡ Basket (optional)

✡ Hot-glue gun (optional)

Instructions

1. Cut plastic canvas according to graphs (below and page 134).

2. Stitch pieces following graphs, working uncoded background on each accent with bright white Continental Stitches. Overcast with royal blue.

3. When background stitching and Overcasting are completed, for candle flames, work topaz pearl cotton Straight Stitches and light tangerine 6-strand embroidery floss French Knots.

4. Work Aztec gold Straight Stitches at bottom of candles with heavy braid. Work Aztec gold Straight Stitches on letters and on star with medium braid. Work all Aztec gold French Knots with medium braid.

5. Options: Back each piece with self-adhesive magnet strips, glue to a basket, or thread a 6" length of white pearl cotton through center top of each piece for hanging ornaments. ✡

COLOR KEY	
#3 Pearl Cotton	**Yards**
■ Royal blue #797	9
Uncoded backgrounds are bright white #B5200 Continental Stitches	17
⁄ Topaz #725 Straight Stitch	1
6-Strand Embroidery Floss	
● Light tangerine #742 French Knot	1
Heavy (#32) Braid	
▢ Aztec gold #202HL	4
⁄ Aztec gold #202HL Straight Stitch	
Medium (#16) Braid	
⁄ Aztec gold #202HL Straight Stitch	5
● Aztec gold #202HL French Knot	
Color numbers given are for DMC #3 pearl cotton and 6-strand embroidery floss and Kreinik Heavy (#32) Braid and Medium (#16) Braid.	

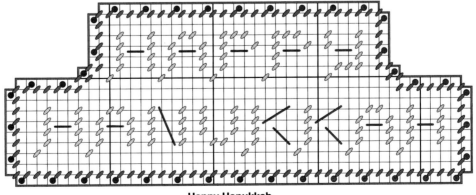

Happy Hanukkah
45 holes x 17 holes
Cut 1

Hanukkah   Hanukkah   Hanukkah   Hanukkah   Hanukkah   Hanukkah

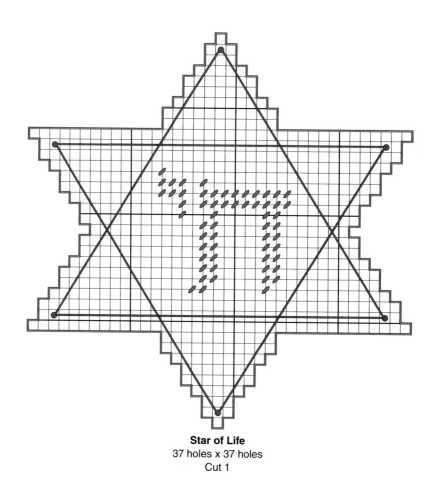

Star of Life
37 holes x 37 holes
Cut 1

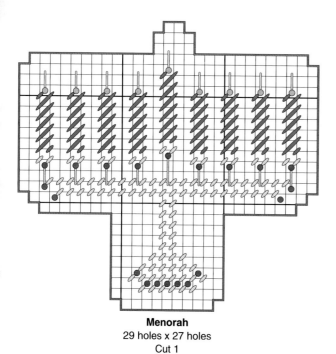

Menorah
29 holes x 27 holes
Cut 1

COLOR KEY

#3 Pearl Cotton	Yards
■ Royal blue #797	9
Uncoded backgrounds are bright white #B5200 Continental Stitches	17
⁄ Topaz #725 Straight Stitch	1
6-Strand Embroidery Floss	
● Light tangerine #742 French Knot	1
Heavy (#32) Braid	
☐ Aztec gold #202HL	4
⁄ Aztec gold #202HL Straight Stitch	
Medium (#16) Braid	
⁄ Aztec gold #202HL Straight Stitch	5
● Aztec gold #202HL French Knot	

Color numbers given are for DMC #3 pearl cotton and 6-strand embroidery floss and Kreinik Heavy (#32) Braid and Medium (#16) Braid.

Hanukkah   Hanukkah   Hanukkah   Hanukkah   Hanukkah   Hanukkah

STAR OF DAVID
Magnet

Design by Angie Arickx

Tack notes to your refrigerator with this eye-catching Star of David magnet!

Skill Level: Beginner

Finished Size

3⅝" W x 4¼" H

Materials

✡ 5" plastic canvas hexagon by Uniek

✡ Uniek Needloft plastic canvas yarn as listed in color key

✡ ⅛"-wide Plastic Canvas 7 Metallic Needlepoint Yarn by Rainbow Gallery as listed in color key

✡ #18 tapestry needle

✡ 1" 1½"-wide magnet strip

Instructions

1. Cut plastic canvas according to graph, cutting away gray area.

2. Stitch piece following graph. Overcast with dark royal.

3. Center and glue magnet strip to backside of stitched star. ✡

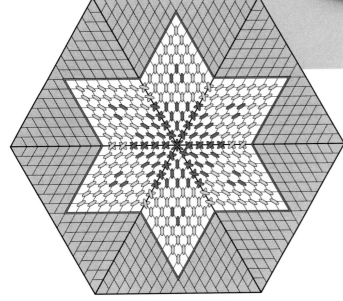

Star of David Magnet
Cut 1
Cut away gray area

COLOR KEY	
Plastic Canvas Yarn	**Yards**
■ Dark royal #48	7
╱ Dark royal #48 Straight Stitch	
⅛" Metallic Needlepoint Yarn	
☐ Silver #PC2	3
Color numbers given are for Uniek Needloft plastic canvas yarn and Rainbow Gallery Plastic Canvas 7 Metallic Needlepoint Yarn.	

Hanukkah   Hanukkah   Hanukkah   Hanukkah   Hanukkah   Hanukkah

ST. NICK
Pillow Topper

Design by Joan Green

This jolly pillow is just what Santa Claus ordered to add a cheery and festive touch to your living room decor!

Skill Level: Beginner

Finished Size

9¼" W x 10⅝" H

Materials

- ½ sheet 7-count plastic canvas
- Spinrite Bernat Berella "4" worsted weight yarn as listed in color key
- ⅛"-wide Plastic Canvas 7 Metallic Needlepoint Yarn by Rainbow Gallery as listed in color key
- #16 tapestry needle
- 38 (4mm) pearl beads
- Sewing needle and white sewing thread
- Aleene's Tack-It Over and Over repositionable glue
- Large forest green pillow

Instructions

1. Cut plastic canvas according to graphs (below and page 138).

2. Stitch pieces following graphs, working beard, mustache and eyebrows with a double strand of white for dimension. Use 1½ yard lengths for long stitches on beard. Work uncoded areas on hat with scarlet Continental Stitches and uncoded area on face with light peach Continental Stitches.

3. For nose, work first layer of stitches in one direction, then work top layer in opposite direction.

4. Work French Knots for center of eyes using 2 plies white.

5. With sewing needle and white sewing thread, attach pearl beads where indicated on graph, knotting ends and weaving in to secure.

6. Overcast mustache with white. Overcast cap edges on Santa with scarlet and remaining edges with adjacent colors. Tack mustache in place beneath nose and cheeks with white yarn.

7. Spread repositionable glue in a thin layer on wrong side of Santa, concentrating on outer edges. Allow to dry for 12 or more hours. Center and press in place on pillow.

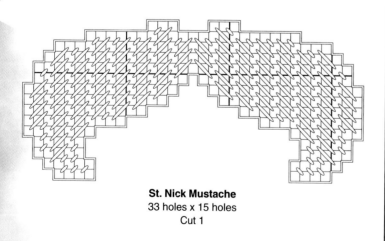

St. Nick Mustache
33 holes x 15 holes
Cut 1

COLOR KEY	
Worsted Weight Yarn	**Yards**
■ Dark lagoon #8822	4
▨ Rose #8921	1
▨ Scarlet #8933	10
□ White #8942	60
■ Navy #8965	½
Uncoded areas on hat are scarlet #8933 Continental Stitches	
Uncoded area on face is light peach #8977 Continental Stitches	5
○ White #8942 French Knot	
⅛" Metallic Needlepoint Yarn	
□ Gold #PC1	2
□ White #PC25	7
● Attach pearl bead	
Color numbers given are for Spinrite Bernat Berella "4" worsted weight yarn and Rainbow Gallery Plastic Canvas 7 Metallic Needlepoint Yarn.	

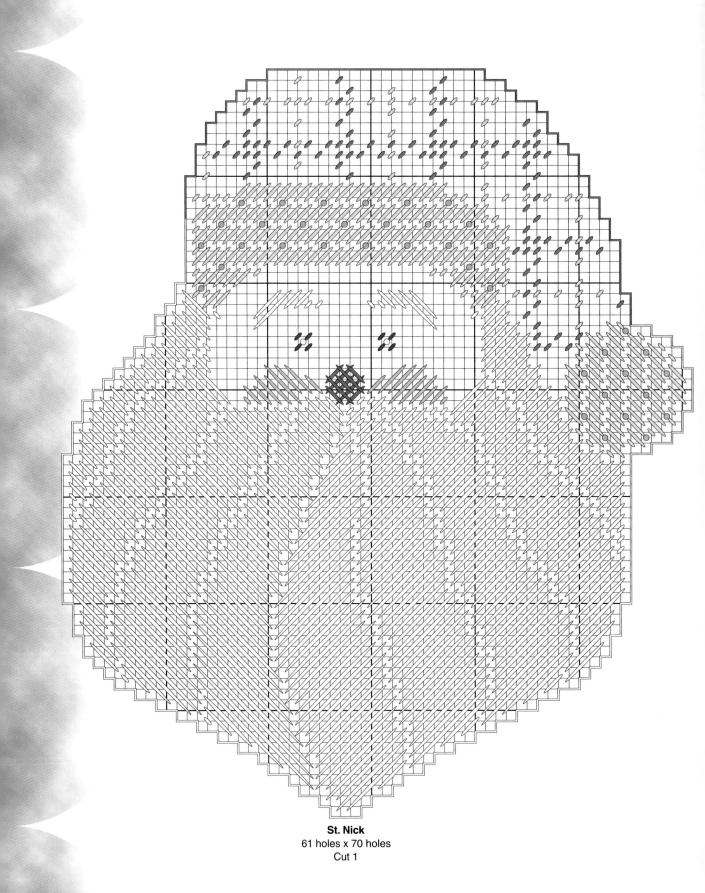

St. Nick
61 holes x 70 holes
Cut 1

Christmas   Christmas   Christmas   Christmas   Christmas   Christmas

SNOWMEN
Centerpiece

Design by Vicki Blizzard

*Bring smiles to the faces of your family members young and
old with this delightful snowmen centerpiece decoration.*

Christmas   Christmas   Christmas   Christmas   Christmas   Christmas

Skill Level: Intermediate

Finished Size

Approximately 10" W x 18" H x 4" D

Materials

- 2 sheets Uniek Quick-Count clear 7-count plastic canvas
- ½ sheet Uniek Quick-Count black 7-count plastic canvas
- Uniek Needloft plastic canvas yarn as listed in color key
- DMC #3 pearl cotton as listed in color key
- #16 tapestry needle
- 2 yards gold #GD2C Gold Rush 18 thin metallic cord from Rainbow Gallery
- 3½" x 4" x 10" basswood carving block #4112 from Walnut Hollow
- Delta Ceramcoat opaque blue #2508 acrylic paint
- Delta Ceramcoat Gleams orange pearl #2617 acrylic paint
- Delta Ceramcoat satin interior varnish
- 1" paintbrush
- ¼" paintbrush
- Fine sandpaper
- Wet paper towel
- White buttons in assorted sizes
- 10 buttons in assorted sizes and colors
- 9 (4mm) round black cabochons from The Beadery
- 7 (5mm) round black cabochons from The Beadery
- 2 (6mm) round black cabochons from The Beadery
- 2 (7mm) round black cabochons from The Beadery
- 3 craft picks or bamboo skewers

- 4" x 10" piece royal blue felt
- 2" x 10" piece green and black checked fabric
- 2" x 10" piece yellow print fabric
- 24" x 8" piece blue and white print fabric
- 3 (5") white battery-powered candles #141-322-07 from National Artcraft
- 3 (9mm) brown chenille stems
- Jewel glue
- Hot-glue gun

Base

1. Sand block to remove rough spots. Wipe away sanding residue with wet paper towel.

2. With 1" brush, paint block with two coats opaque blue acrylic paint, allowing to dry thoroughly between coats.

3. When second coat of paint is dry, glue white buttons as desired to front, back, sides and top of base with jewel glue, making sure to leave room on base top for snowmen.

4. Apply two coats of varnish to block, allowing to dry thoroughly between coats.

5. Attach royal blue felt to bottom of block with hot glue.

6. Tear a 1" x 24" strip of blue and white print fabric. Using photo as a guide, wrap fabric strip around base, knotting in front. Secure with hot glue.

7. Tear three 1½" x 9" strips of blue and white print fabric. Place strips together and tie a knot in center to form a bow. Glue bow over knot on fabric strip.

Noses

1. Using ¼" paintbrush, paint 1" of pointed ends on craft picks or bamboo skewers with two coats of orange pearl paint. Allow to dry between coats.

2. When dry, cut off painted ends. Set aside.

Snowmen

1. Cut all hat tops and hat brims from black plastic canvas; cut snowmen fronts, backs, sides and mittens from clear plastic canvas according to graphs (pages 141–143).

2. Stitch pieces following graphs, reversing two of each snowman's mittens before stitching.

3. Overcast outside edges of hat brims with black. Do not Overcast inside edges of hat brims and hat tops.

4. Whipstitch corresponding snowmen fronts, backs and sides together with adjacent colors. With black, Whipstitch corresponding hat tops to each snowman. Overcast bottom edges with white.

5. Slide corresponding hat brims over tops of each snowman to where black stitching meets white stitching.

6. Cut chenille stems in half. Matching edges and using adjacent colors, Whipstitch wrong sides of mitten pairs together, sliding one end of a chenille stem between wrist area of mittens while Whipstitching.

7. Using photo as a guide, determine arm placement for each snowman. Carefully separate stitching and insert remaining end of chenille stem into hole. Push end through until arm is desired length, then reach inside snowman and fold excess chenille stem tightly against body. Bend each chenille stem to form

Christmas   Christmas   Christmas   Christmas   Christmas   Christmas

elbows. *Note: Thumbs of mittens should be on top.*

Signs & Heart

1. Cut signs and heart from clear plastic canvas according to graphs.

2. Stitch pieces following graphs, working pearl cotton embroidery on signs when background stitching is completed.

3. Overcast following graphs.

Finishing

1. Use photo as a guide throughout finishing. For small snowman, tear green and black checked fabric into a ½" x 10" strip for scarf, then cut or tear a ½" x 2" piece.

2. Tie scarf around neck where white Continental Stitches and Slanting Gobelin Stitches meet on front. Cut a ½" fringe on each end. Tie a knot in center of ½" x

2" piece to form a bow. Trim ends and glue to base of crown on hat.

3. With jewel glue, attach two 5mm cabochons to face for eyes and four 4mm cabochons to face for mouth. Push cut end of painted craft pick or bamboo skewer into center of face for nose. Glue three different colored buttons to front of snowman below scarf.

4. For medium snowman, tear blue and white print fabric into a 1" x 12" strip for scarf, then cut or tear a 1" x 3" piece for bow.

5. Following steps 2 and 3 throughout, attach scarf and bow. Use two 6mm cabochons for eyes and remaining five 4mm cabochons for mouth.

6. For large snowman, tear yellow print fabric into a 1" x 9" strip. Fold in half lengthwise with wrong sides together, then

wrap around crown of hat to form hatband; glue ends in place on backside. Glue one button to hatband. Tear a 1" x 4" strip and tie a knot in center to form bow. Trim ends and glue to front of snowman at neck.

7. Follow step 3 to form face, using 7mm cabochons for eyes and remaining five 5mm cabochons for mouth.

8. Glue snowmen in position on base top. Insert one candle in top opening of each hat.

9. Cut gold thin metallic cord into six equal lengths. Tie a loop in one end of each length. Thread remaining ends through back of signs and heart at top corners, making lengths approximately 2" long. Place loops over mittens on snowmen so message reads "I ♥ SNOW." Adjust position of arms as desired. 🎁

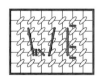

"We" Sign
8 holes x 6 holes
Cut 1 from clear

COLOR KEY

Plastic Canvas Yarn	Yards
■ Black #00	39
■ Christmas red #02	6
■ Holly #27	4
□ White #41	102
□ Yellow #57	4
⁄ Royal #32 Overcasting	1
#3 Pearl Cotton	
⁄ Christmas green #699 Backstitch	1
⁄ Royal blue #797 Backstitch	1

Color numbers given are for Uniek Needloft plastic canvas yarn and DMC #3 pearl cotton.

"Snow" Sign
15 holes x 7 holes
Cut 1

Heart
13 holes x 13 holes
Cut 1 from clear

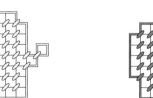

Large Snowman Mitten
6 holes x 8 holes
Cut 4, reverse 2, from clear

Medium Snowman Mitten
6 holes x 7 holes
Cut 4, reverse 2, from clear

Small Snowman Mitten
5 holes x 7 holes
Cut 4, reverse 2, from clear

Christmas   Christmas   Christmas   Christmas   Christmas   Christmas

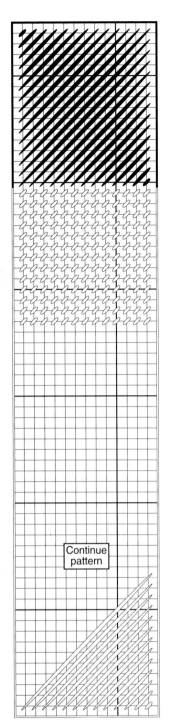

Large Snowman Front
14 holes x 65 holes
Cut 1 from clear

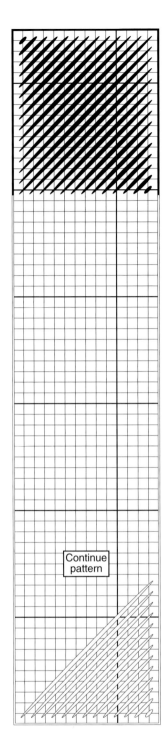

Large Snowman Back & Side
14 holes x 65 holes
Cut 3 from clear

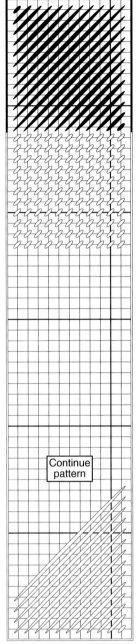

Medium Snowman Front
12 holes x 60 holes
Cut 1 from clear

COLOR KEY	
Plastic Canvas Yarn	**Yards**
■ Black #00	39
■ Christmas red #02	6
■ Holly #27	4
□ White #41	102
□ Yellow #57	4
∕ Royal #32 Overcasting	1
#3 Pearl Cotton	
∕ Christmas green #699 Backstitch	1
∕ Royal blue #797 Backstitch	1
Color numbers given are for Uniek Needloft plastic canvas yarn and DMC #3 pearl cotton.	

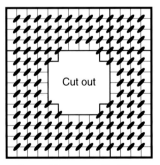

Large Snowman Hat Top
14 holes x 14 holes
Cut 1 from black

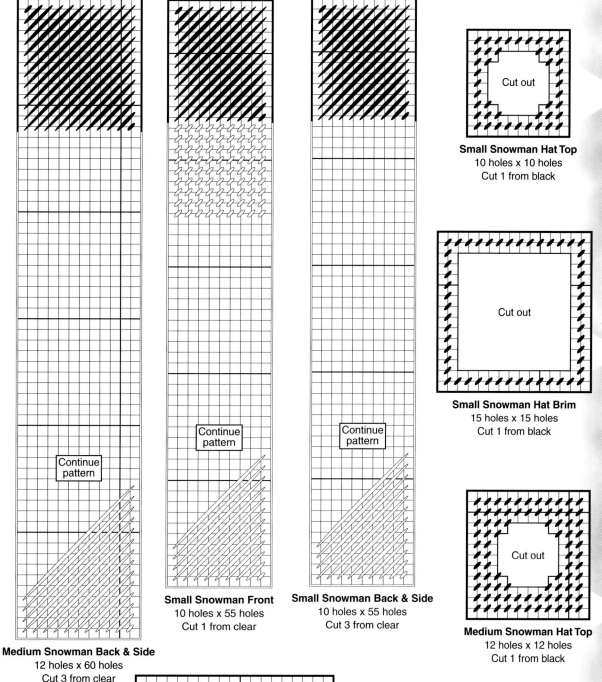

Medium Snowman Back & Side
12 holes x 60 holes
Cut 3 from clear

Small Snowman Front
10 holes x 55 holes
Cut 1 from clear

Small Snowman Back & Side
10 holes x 55 holes
Cut 3 from clear

Continue pattern

Continue pattern

Continue pattern

Cut out

Small Snowman Hat Top
10 holes x 10 holes
Cut 1 from black

Cut out

Small Snowman Hat Brim
15 holes x 15 holes
Cut 1 from black

Cut out

Medium Snowman Hat Top
12 holes x 12 holes
Cut 1 from black

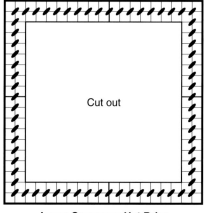

Cut out

Large Snowman Hat Brim
19 holes x 19 holes
Cut 1 from black

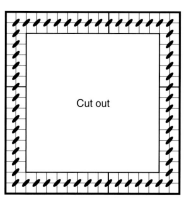

Cut out

Medium Snowman Hat Brim
17 holes x 17 holes
Cut 1 from black

Christmas   Christmas   Christmas   Christmas   Christmas   Christmas

CHRISTMAS
Ornament Cuties

Designs by Janelle Giese

Stitched with soft chenille yarn and designed with oodles of personality, these sweet ornaments are cute enough to hug!

Skill Level: Beginner

Finished Size

Santa: 4" W x 4⅝" H
Angel: 3½" W x 4⅝" H
Bear: 3⅜" W x 4¼" H

Materials

🎁 ⅔ sheet 7-count plastic canvas

🎁 Lion Chenille Sensations acrylic yarn from Lion Brand Yarn Co. as listed in color key

🎁 Kreinik ⅛" Ribbon as listed in color key

🎁 DMC 6-strand embroidery floss as listed in color key

🎁 DMC #5 pearl cotton as listed in color key

🎁 DMC #8 pearl cotton as listed in color key

🎁 #16 tapestry needle

🎁 Hot-glue gun or craft glue

Pattern Notes

Work with 18" lengths of chenille yarn.

Work white and lighter colors first, then dark shades.

Instructions

1. Cut plastic canvas according to graphs (on this page and page 146).

2. Stitch pieces following graphs, working uncoded areas on Santa and angel with white Continental Stitches and uncoded areas on bear with sandstone Continental Stitches.

3. Overcast Santa with adjacent colors. Overcast halo on angel with gold ⅛" ribbon and remaining edges with adjacent colors.

Overcast bear with sandstone.

4. For Santa, embroider belt buckle with gold ⅛" ribbon. Work cheeks with 2 strands salmon embroidery floss. Work remaining features with black #5 pearl cotton, stitching each eye with four vertical stitches. *Note: Do not stitch wrinkles in corners of eyes four times.*

5. For angel, work Straight Stitches for hearts on bottom of skirt with red yarn. Using two strands embroidery floss, work cheeks with salmon, curlicues on skirt with Christmas green and Cross Stitches on wings with pale delft.

6. With gold ⅛" ribbon, work Straight Stitches on halo and French knots on sleeves and skirt. Embroider remaining fea-

tures with black #8 pearl cotton, working eyes as in step 4.

7. For bear, work black #5 pearl cotton Backstitches and Straight Stitches, stitching each eye with four vertical stitches.

8. Work a red yarn Straight Stitch for tongue and a forest green yarn Straight Stitch for ribbon on package. For bow, thread a 6" length of forest green yarn from front to back through holes indicated on graph. Tie yarn in a bow; trim ends. Secure bow with a dab of glue.

9. For hangers, cut a 7" length of black #8 pearl cotton for each ornament. Thread ends from front to back where indicated on graphs. Tie a knot on backside, making a 3" loop. Trim ends. 🎁

COLOR KEY
BEAR

Chenille Acrylic Yarn	Yards
☐ Antique white #98	2
■ Red #112	1
■ Black #153	1
Uncoded areas are sandstone #155 Continental Stitches	8
✎ Sandstone #155 Overcasting	
✎ Red #112 Straight Stitch	
✎ Forest green #131 Straight Stitch	1
⅛" Ribbon	
▨ Gold #002HL	1
#5 Pearl Cotton	
✎ Black #310 Backstitch and Straight Stitch	3
● Attach hanger	
● Attach bow	

Color numbers given are for Lion Brand Lion Chenille Sensations acrylic yarn, Kreinik ⅛" Ribbon and DMC 6-strand embroidery floss and #5 pearl cotton.

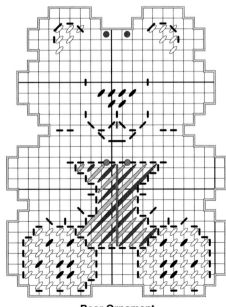

Bear Ornament
21 holes x 27 holes
Cut 1

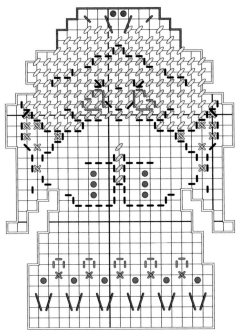

Angel Ornament
22 holes x 30 holes
Cut 1

COLOR KEY
ANGEL

Chenille Acrylic Yarn		Yards
☐	Natural #123	2
☐	Yellow #157	2
	Uncoded areas are white #100 Continental Stitches	8
∕	White #100 Overcasting	
∕	Red #112 Straight Stitch	1

⅛" Ribbon

∕	Gold #002HL Straight Stitch and Overcasting	
●	Gold #002HL French Knot	

6-Strand Embroidery Floss

∕	Christmas green #699 Backstitch	1
✖	Christmas green #699 Cross Stitch	
✖	Pale delft #800 Cross Stitch	1
∕	Dark salmon #3328 Backstitch	1

#8 Pearl Cotton

∕	Black #310 Backstitch and Straight Stitch	3
●	Attach hanger	

Color numbers given are for Lion Brand Lion Chenille Sensations acrylic yarn, Kreinik ⅛" Ribbon and DMC 6-strand embroidery floss and #5 pearl cotton.

Santa Ornament
25 holes x 30 holes
Cut 1

COLOR KEY
SANTA

Chenille Acrylic Yarn		Yards
■	Red #112	3
☐	Natural #123	1
■	Forest green #131	1
■	Black #153	2
	Uncoded areas are white #100 Continental Stitches	5
∕	White #100 Overcasting	

⅛" Ribbon

∕	Gold #002HL Backstitch	1

6-Strand Embroidery Floss

✖	Dark salmon #3328 Cross Stitch	1

#5 Pearl Cotton

∕	Black #310 Backstitch and Straight Stitch	3
●	Black #310 French Knot	
○	Attach hanger	

Color numbers given are for Lion Brand Lion Chenille Sensations acrylic yarn, Kreinik ⅛" Ribbon and DMC 6-strand embroidery floss and #5 pearl cotton.

Christmas   Christmas   Christmas   Christmas   Christmas   Christmas

CHRISTMAS
Fridgie Frame

Design by Angie Arickx

Send a favorite family snapshot to Grandma and Grandpa in this plastic canvas greeting!

Skill Level: Beginner

Finished Size
6¼" W x 5" H

Materials

- ⅓ sheet Uniek Quick-Count 7-count plastic canvas
- Uniek Needloft plastic canvas yarn as listed in color key
- #16 tapestry needle
- 4" x 5" piece adhesive-backed magnetic sheet

Instructions

1. Cut plastic canvas according to graphs.

2. Stitch pieces following graphs, working uncoded areas on frame with white Continental Stitches. Add red Straight Stitches to letters on frame when background stitching is completed. Do not work yellow Straight Stitches on poinsettias at this time.

3. Overcast poinsettias with red. Overcast inside edges on frame with white and outside edges with holly and white following graph.

4. Place one poinsettia on each frame corner

where indicated on graph and attach with yellow Straight Stitches in center of poinsettia, working through both layers of plastic canvas.

5. Cut an oval in center of magnetic sheet larger than oval in frame. Peel off adhesive backing and attach to backside of frame.

Fridgie Frame Poinsettia
7 holes x 7 holes
Cut 4

COLOR KEY	
Plastic Canvas Yarn	**Yards**
■ Red #01	7
▨ Holly #27	3
Uncoded areas are white #41	
Continental Stitches	12
⁄ White #41 Overcasting	
⁄ Red #01 Straight Stitch	
⁄ Yellow #57 Backstitch	1
● Attach poinsettia	
Color numbers given are for Uniek Needloft plastic canvas yarn.	

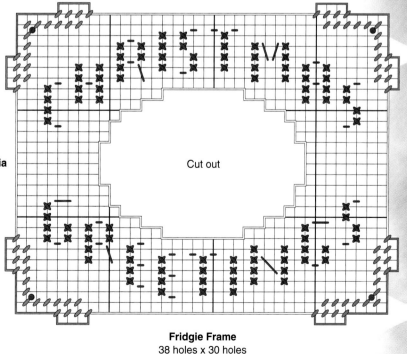

Cut out

Fridgie Frame
38 holes x 30 holes
Cut 1

CHRISTMAS FRIDGIE FRAME • **147**

Christmas   Christmas   Christmas   Christmas   Christmas   Christmas

BOUGHS OF HOLLY
Place Mat

Design by Kathleen Hurley

*Make each place setting at Christmas dinner extra special by stitching
one of these beautiful place mats for each guest!*

Skill Level: Beginner

Finished Size

18" W x 12" H

Materials

- 12" x 18" white 7-count oval sheet plastic canvas from Darice
- Uniek Needloft plastic canvas yarn as listed in color key
- Uniek metallic craft cord as listed in color key
- #16 tapestry needle

Instructions

1. Following graph, work leaves with fern, holly and forest, doubling yarn for Long Stitches where indicated.

2. For holly berries, work each large Christmas red Cross Stitch in center first, then work small stitches over the four corners of Cross Stitch.

3. Work gold metallic cord Backstitches and Straight Stitches.

COLOR KEY	
Plastic Canvas Yarn	**Yards**
■ Christmas red #02	5
□ Fern #23	10
▢ Holly #27	10
■ Forest #29	11
Metallic Craft Cord	
╱ Gold #02 Backstitch and Straight Stitch	5
Color numbers given are for Uniek Needloft plastic canvas yarn and metallic craft cord.	

Christmas   Christmas   Christmas   Christmas   Christmas   Christmas

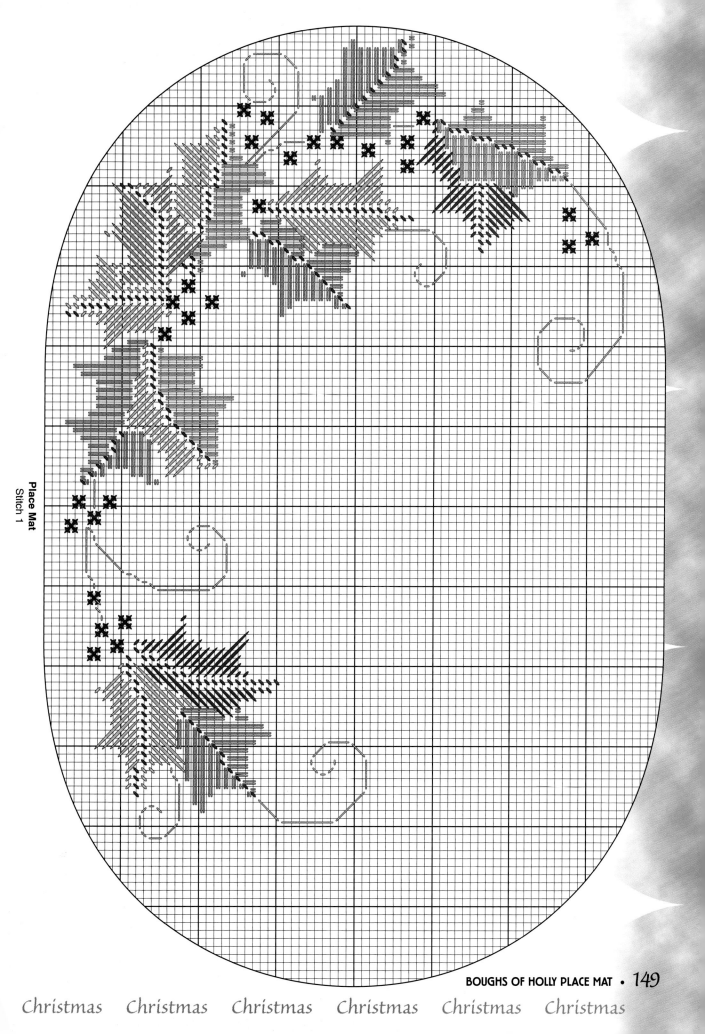

Place Mat
Stitch 1

Christmas   Christmas   Christmas   Christmas   Christmas   Christmas

SNOWMAN
Door Hanger

Design by Kathleen Hurley

Holding a sack filled with colorful gifts, this friendly snowman will add a welcoming touch to your front door!

Skill Level: Beginner

Finished Size

5⅜" W x 12⅞" H

Materials

- 1 sheet 7-count plastic canvas
- Uniek Needloft plastic canvas yarn as listed in color key
- DMC #3 pearl cotton as listed in color key
- #16 tapestry needle
- 33 (3.5mm) pearl beads
- Sewing needle and white sewing thread

Instructions

1. Cut plastic canvas according to graph.

2. Stitch piece following graph, working uncoded areas with white Continental Stitches.

3. When background stitching is completed, use black pearl cotton to work Backstitches for snowman's mouth and French Knot for bird's eye. Work straw Straight Stitches for bird's feet.

4. For scarf fringe, work holly Lark's Head Knots where indicated on graph. Unravel ends and trim to desired length.

5. With sewing needle and white sewing thread, attach beads where indicated on graph.

6. Overcast with bright blue and white following graph.

COLOR KEY

Plastic Canvas Yarn	Yards
■ Black #00	4
■ Red #01	5
■ Pink #07	2
■ Maple #13	2
□ Straw #19	1
■ Holly #27	10
■ Silver #37	1
■ Bittersweet #52	1
□ Yellow #57	1
□ White #41	13
■ Bright blue #60	25

Uncoded areas are white #41
Continental Stitches

⁄ Straw #19 Straight Stitch
● Holly #27 Lark's Head Knot

#3 Pearl Cotton

⁄ Black #310 Backstitch	1
● Black #310 French Knot	
● Attach pearl bead	

Color numbers given are for Uniek Needloft
plastic canvas yarn and DMC #3 pearl cotton.

Door Hanger
35 holes x 85 holes
Cut 1

CHRISTMAS TREATS
Spoon Toppers

Designs by Joan Green

Here's a unique Christmas kitchen decoration—dressed up wooden spoons! Tie them together with a bow and prop them in a corner or stand them up in a decorative jar!

Skill Level: Beginner

Finished Size
Frosted Cookie: 3½" W x 3" H
Gingerbread Boy: 2⅞" W x 3⅜" H
Plum Pudding: 2⅞" W x 3¼" H

Materials
- ½ sheet 7-count plastic canvas
- Spinrite Bernat Berella "4" worsted weight yarn as listed in color key
- #16 tapestry needle
- Mill Hill Products beads from Gay Bowles Sales Inc.:
  8 red velvet #72052 small bugle beads
  14 Christmas green #00167 glass seed beads

8 ruby #05025 glass pebble beads

- Beading needle and sewing thread
- 3 wooden spoons
- Needle-nose pliers

Instructions
1. Cut front and back pieces from plastic canvas according to graphs. Backs will remain unstitched.

2. Stitch front pieces following graphs, working uncoded area on frosted cookie with pale tapestry gold Continental Stitches, uncoded area on plum pudding with warm brown Continental Stitches and uncoded areas on gingerbread boy with honey Continental Stitches.

3. When background stitching is completed, work warm brown French Knots and Backstitches on gingerbread boy.

4. With beading needle and sewing thread, attach all beads where indicated on frosted cookie and plum pudding graphs, knotting thread ends and weaving in to secure.

5. Overcast bottom edges on front pieces between dots with adjacent colors. Whipstitch fronts to backs along all remaining edges following graphs.

6. Insert spoon handles into bottom openings of toppers.

COLOR KEY
FROSTED COOKIE

Worsted Weight Yarn		Yards
■ Honey #8795		4
Uncoded areas are pale tapestry gold #8887 Continental Stitches		2
⁄ Attach red velvet bugle bead		
○ Attach Christmas green seed bead		
● Attach ruby pebble bead		

Color numbers given are for Spinrite Bernat Berella "4" worsted weight yarn.

Frosted Cookie
22 holes x 19 holes
Cut 2, stitch 1

COLOR KEY
GINGERBREAD BOY

Worsted Weight Yarn		Yards
■ Warm brown #8797		½
■ Dark lagoon #8822		2
■ Rose #8921		½
■ Scarlet #8933		3
□ White #8942		½
Uncoded areas are honey #8795 Continental Stitches		5
⁄ Honey #8795 Overcasting and Whipstitching		
⁄ Warm brown #8797 Backstitch		
● Warm brown #8797 French Knot		

Color numbers given are for Spinrite Bernat Berella "4" worsted weight yarn.

Christmas   Christmas   Christmas   Christmas   Christmas   Christmas

Plum Pudding
18 holes x 21 holes
Cut 2, stitch 1

COLOR KEY
PLUM PUDDING

Worsted Weight Yarn	Yards
☐ Medium lagoon #8821	1
■ Dark lagoon #8822	2
☐ Pale tapestry gold #8887	½
■ Scarlet #8933	½
☐ White #8942	3
Uncoded areas are warm brown #8797 Continental Stitches	4
╱ Warm brown #8797 Overcasting and Whipstitching	
● Attach ruby pebble bead	

Color numbers given are for Spinrite Bernat Berella "4" worsted weight yarn.

Gingerbread Boy
18 holes x 22 holes
Cut 2, stitch 1

Christmas   Christmas   Christmas   Christmas   Christmas   Christmas

SANTA BEAR
in the Chimney

Design by Angie Arickx

Look who has just slid down the chimney—it's Santa bear! Tuck this delightful knick-knack on a favorite shelf for Christmas cheer!

Skill Level: Beginner

Finished Size

3⅝" W x 2¾"H x1¼" D

Materials

- ¼ sheet Uniek Quick-Count 7-count plastic canvas
- Small amount 10-Count plastic canvas
- Uniek Needloft plastic canvas yarn as listed in color key
- DMC #3 pearl cotton as listed in color key
- #16 tapestry needle
- #18 tapestry needle
- 1½" brown flocked Santa bear
- Hot-glue gun

Instructions

1. Cut three stockings from 10-count plastic canvas; cut all fireplace pieces from 7-count plastic canvas according to graphs.

2. With #18 tapestry needle and #3 pearl cotton, stitch and Overcast stockings following graphs, working one with medium topaz as graphed, one with medium carnation and one with medium emerald green.

3. With #16 tapestry needle and yarn, stitch fireplace pieces following graphs, working uncoded areas on fireplace front, sides and top with white Continental Stitches. Work embroidery when background stitching is completed.

4. Using brown throughout, Overcast front edge of fireplace bottom from dot to dot. Whipstitch fireplace back to back edge of fireplace bottom.

5. Using white throughout, Overcast opening edges on fireplace front. Whipstitch fireplace sides and front to fireplace bottom. Whipstitch sides to front and back, then Whipstitch top to front, back and sides.

6. Using photo as a guide, glue Santa bear inside fireplace opening to bottom piece; glue stockings to fireplace front.

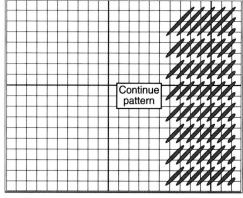

Fireplace Back
23 holes x 18 holes
Cut 1 from 7-count

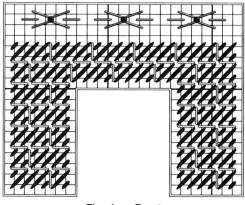

Fireplace Front
23 holes x 18 holes
Cut 1 from 7-count

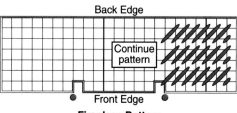

Fireplace Bottom
23 holes x 7 holes
Cut 1 from 7-count

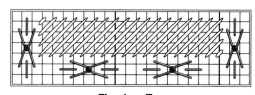

Fireplace Top
23 holes x 7 holes
Cut 1 from 7-count

Christmas   Christmas   Christmas   Christmas   Christmas   Christmas

COLOR KEY

Plastic Canvas Yarn	Yards
■ Red #01	6
■ Brown #15	9
□ White #41	12
Uncoded areas are white #41 Continental Stitches	
╱ Christmas green #28 Straight Stitch	
╱ White #41 Backstitch and Straight Stitch	2
● Christmas red #02 French Knot	1
#3 Pearl Cotton	
▨ Medium topaz #783	½
Medium carnation #892	½
Medium emerald green #911	½

Color numbers given are for Uniek Needloft plastic canvas yarn and DMC #3 pearl cotton.

Fireplace Side
7 holes x 18 holes
Cut 2 from 7-count

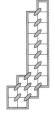

Stocking
4 holes x 10 holes
Cut 3 from 10-count
Stitch 1 as graphed,
1 with medium carnation,
1 with medium emerald green

FURRY FRIENDS
Gift Stockings

Designs by Celia Lange Designs

Pet lovers will get a kick out of these whimsical, miniature puppy and kitty stockings!

Skill Level: Beginner

Finished Size
Kitty: 5⅜" W x 6½" H
Puppy: 5⅜" W x 6⅜" H

Materials
- 1 sheet regular 7-count plastic canvas
- ¼ sheet Darice Ultra Stiff 7-count plastic canvas
- Coats & Clark Red Heart Classic worsted weight yarn Art. E267 as listed in color key
- DMC #3 pearl cotton as listed in color key
- #16 tapestry needle
- 2 (7mm) blue round movable eyes
- 2 (10mm) black oval movable eyes
- 2 (¼") white pompoms
- Hot-glue gun

Instructions

1. Cut puppy and kitty heads from stiff plastic canvas; cut all remaining pieces from regular plastic canvas according to graphs (below and page 158).

2. Stitch pieces following graphs, reversing one of each stocking before stitching. Work uncoded area on kitty head with nickel Continental Stitches and uncoded area on puppy head with warm brown Continental Stitches.

3. When Continental Stitching is completed on stocking fronts and backs, work topaz and ecru pearl cotton embroidery on stocking fronts only.

4. Overcast heads, paws and hatbands with adjacent colors. Work black pearl cotton embroidery on heads and paws when stitching and Overcasting are completed.

5. Using adjacent colors and matching edges, Whipstitch wrong sides of corresponding stocking pieces together around side and bottom edges; Overcast top edges.

6. Using white throughout, Overcast top and bottom edges of stocking cuffs. Whipstitch wrong sides of two stocking cuffs together along side edges. Repeat with remaining two stocking cuff pieces.

7. For each hanger, cut desired length of white yarn and thread through upper right holes of stocking cuffs. Knot on inside.

8. Using photo as a guide through step 9, slide cuff over stockings until top edges are even; glue in place.

9. Glue hatbands to corresponding heads. Glue blue movable eyes to kitty's face and black movable eyes to dog's face. Glue pompoms to tips of hats. Glue heads and paws to stockings.

COLOR KEY	
KITTY	
Worsted Weight Yarn	**Yards**
☐ White #01	7
▨ Nickel #401	4
▦ Paddy green #686	2
■ Cherry red #912	20
Uncoded area on kitty head is nickel #401 Continental Stitches	
#3 Pearl Cotton	
✎ Black #310 Backstitch and Straight Stitch	1
✎ Topaz #725 Backstitch	3
Color numbers given are for Red Heart Classic worsted weight yarn Art. E267 and DMC #3 pearl cotton.	

Kitty Hatband
10 holes x 2 holes
Cut 1 from regular

Stocking Cuff
19 holes x 9 holes
Cut 4 from regular

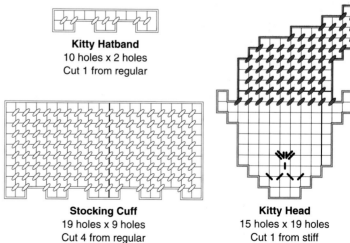

Kitty Head
15 holes x 19 holes
Cut 1 from stiff

Christmas   Christmas   Christmas   Christmas   Christmas   Christmas

COLOR KEY
KITTY

Worsted Weight Yarn	Yards
☐ White #01	7
▨ Nickel #401	4
▨ Paddy green #686	2
■ Cherry red #912	20

Uncoded area on kitty head is
nickel #401 Continental Stitches

#3 Pearl Cotton

✔ Black #310 Backstitch and Straight Stitch	1
✔ Topaz #725 Backstitch	3

Color numbers given are for Red Heart Classic
worsted weight yarn Art. E267 and DMC #3
pearl cotton.

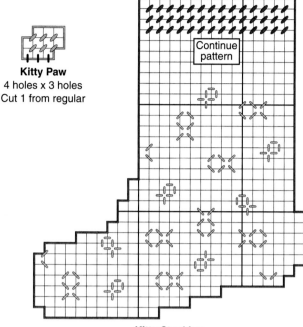

Kitty Paw
4 holes x 3 holes
Cut 1 from regular

Kitty Stocking
26 holes x 30 holes
Cut 2, reverse 1, from regular

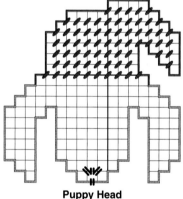

Puppy Head
17 holes x 17 holes
Cut 1 from stiff

Puppy Hatband
12 holes x 2 holes
Cut 1 from regular

COLOR KEY
PUPPY

Worsted Weight Yarn	Yards
☐ White #01	7
▨ Warm brown #336	4
▨ Paddy green #686	20
■ Cherry red #912	2

Uncoded area on puppy head
is warm brown #336
Continental Stitches

#3 Pearl Cotton

✔ Ecru Straight Stitch	4
✔ Black #310 Backstitch and Straight Stitch	1
○ Ecru French Knot	

Color numbers given are for Red Heart Classic
worsted weight yarn Art. E267 and DMC #3
pearl cotton.

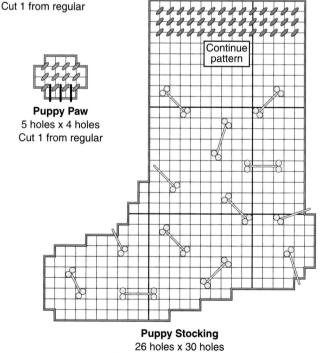

Puppy Paw
5 holes x 4 holes
Cut 1 from regular

Puppy Stocking
26 holes x 30 holes
Cut 2, reverse 1, from regular

Christmas Christmas Christmas Christmas Christmas Christmas

Design by Angie Arickx

Filled with your favorite candy treats, this pretty candy dish is festive and fun!

Skill Level: Beginner

Finished Size

5½" W x 5⅛" H x 1¾" D

Materials

- 2 (5") Uniek plastic canvas stars
- ¼ sheet Uniek Quick-Count 7-count plastic canvas
- Uniek Needloft plastic canvas yarn as listed in color key
- #16 tapestry needle

Instructions

1. Cut plastic canvas according to graphs (page 160).

2. Stitch pieces following graphs. Work yellow French Knots on front and back when background stitching is completed.

3. Using white throughout, Overcast top edges of front and back from dot to dot. Whipstitch side pieces together, forming one long strip; Whipstitch sides to front and back around side and bottom edges from dot to dot. Overcast top edges of sides.

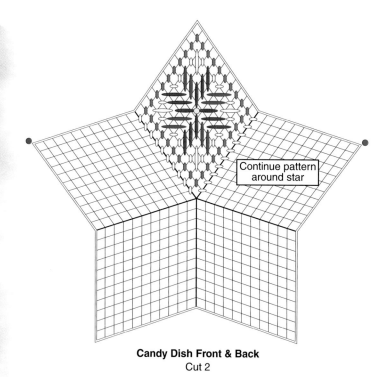

Continue pattern around star

Candy Dish Front & Back
Cut 2

Candy Dish Side
11 holes x 11 holes
Cut 6

COLOR KEY	
Plastic Canvas Yarn	**Yards**
■ Red #01	5
■ Christmas red #02	8
■ Holly #27	14
☐ White #41	16
○ Yellow #57 French Knot	1
Color numbers given are for Uniek Needloft plastic canvas yarn.	

Designs by Angie Arickx

Hang this pair of diminutive bears on your Christmas tree for a sweet, handstitched accent!

Skill Level: Beginner

Finished Size

Each basket: 2" W x 2⅝" H x 1" D

Materials

- ¼ sheet Uniek Quick-Count 7-count plastic canvas
- Uniek Needloft plastic canvas yarn as listed in color key
- #16 tapestry needle
- 2 (1") flocked bears: 1 white and 1 brown
- Hot-glue gun

Instructions

1. For each basket, cut one basket front, one basket back and one basket sides and handle from plastic canvas according to graphs (page 162). Cut one 7-hole x 5-hole piece for each basket bottom.

2. Stitch one basket following graphs. Work Christmas red Backstitches on basket front only when background stitching is completed. Overcast handle edges alternating Christmas red with white. Continental Stitch one basket bottom with maple,

and one basket bottom with tan.

3. Overcast pieces with Christmas green where indicated on graphs. Using maple, Whipstitch basket front and back to basket sides, then Whipstitch front, back and sides to basket bottom.

4. Stitch remaining basket following steps 2 and 3, replacing maple with tan, Christmas green with forest, Christmas red with crimson and white with eggshell.

5. Using photo as a guide, glue white bear inside maple basket and brown bear inside tan basket.

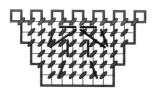

Basket Front & Back
13 holes x 7 holes
Cut 2 for each basket
Stitch 2 as graphed
Stitch 2, replacing maple with tan,
Christmas green with forest
and Christmas red with crimson

COLOR KEY	
Plastic Canvas Yarn	**Yards**
■ Christmas red #02	1
▨ Maple #13	4
Tan #18	4
■ Christmas green #28	2
Forest #29	2
Eggshell #39	1
□ White #41	1
Crimson #42	1
✎ Christmas red #02 Backstitch	
Color numbers given are for Uniek Needloft plastic canvas yarn.	

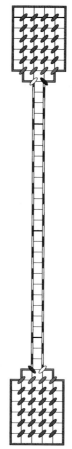

Basket Sides & Handle
5 holes x 41 holes
Cut 1 for each basket
Stitch 1 as graphed
Stitch 1, replacing maple with tan,
Christmas green with forest,
Christmas red with crimson
and white with eggshell

HOLIDAY
Beverage Covers

Design by Kathleen Hurley

Here's a unique gift idea! Give this pair of beverage covers, along with your favorite eggnog or wassail, to a special friend or coworker!

Christmas   Christmas   Christmas   Christmas   Christmas   Christmas

Skill Level: Beginner

Finished Size
3½" H x 3" in diameter

Materials
- 1 sheet 7-count plastic canvas
- 2 (3") plastic canvas radial circles by Darice
- Uniek Needloft plastic canvas yarn as listed in color key
- #16 tapestry needle
- 7 (6mm) dark ruby faceted beads
- Monofilament
- Hot-glue gun

Instructions
1. Cut plastic canvas according to graphs. Do not cut 3" radial circles.

2. Stitch pieces following graphs. Do not stitch vertical bar indicated on each cover side. Work holly Straight Stitches on leaves when background stitching is completed.

3. Using Christmas red, Overlap one hole on holly cover side following graph, placing left end over right end; Whipstitch together with a Continental Stitch. Repeat with candy cane cover side using holly.

4. Overcast leaves with holly and candy canes with Christmas red and white following graph.

5. With Christmas red, Overcast top edge of holly cover side, then Whipstitch bottom edge to holly cover bottom. With holly, Overcast top edge of candy cane cover side, then Whipstitch bottom edge to candy cane bottom.

6. Using monofilament, attach four beads to double holly leaves and three beads to candy cane leaves where indicated on graphs.

7. Using photo as a guide, glue single holly leaf to holly cover, then center and glue double leaves over single leaf. Glue candy canes to candy cane cover, then glue candy cane leaves to candy canes.

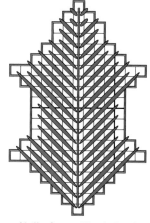

Holly Cover Single Leaf
13 holes x 20 holes
Cut 1

COLOR KEY	
HOLLY BEVERAGE COVER	
Plastic Canvas Yarn	**Yards**
■ Christmas red #02	14
■ Holly #27	8
□ White #41	8
╱ Holly #27 Straight Stitch	
● Attach bead	
Color numbers given are for Uniek Needloft plastic canvas yarn.	

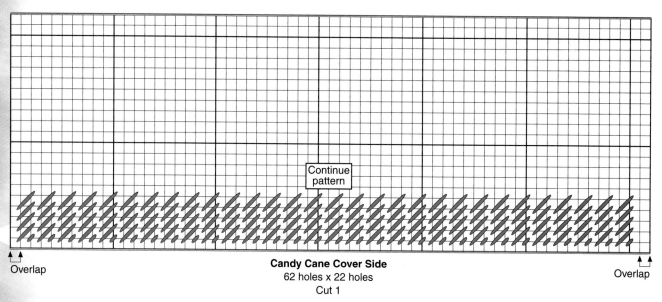

Overlap

Continue pattern

Overlap

Candy Cane Cover Side
62 holes x 22 holes
Cut 1

Christmas   Christmas   Christmas   Christmas   Christmas   Christmas

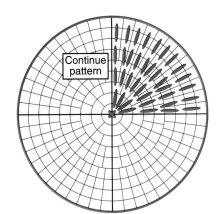

Candy Cane Cover Bottom
Stitch 1 as graphed
Holly Cover Bottom
Stitch 1 with Christmas red

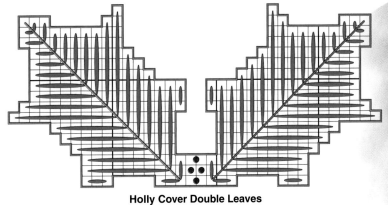

Holly Cover Double Leaves
36 holes x 17 holes
Cut 1

COLOR KEY
HOLLY BEVERAGE COVER

Plastic Canvas Yarn	Yards
■ Christmas red #02	14
■ Holly #27	8
□ White #41	8
╱ Holly #27 Straight Stitch	
● Attach bead	

Color numbers given are for Uniek Needloft plastic canvas yarn.

Candy Cane Cover Leaves
15 holes x 9 holes
Cut 1

COLOR KEY
CANDY CANE BEVERAGE COVER

Plastic Canvas Yarn	Yards
■ Christmas red #02	4
■ Holly #27	28
□ White #41	3
╱ Holly #27 Straight Stitch	
● Attach bead	

Color numbers given are for Uniek Needloft plastic canvas yarn.

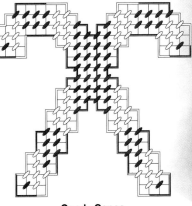

Candy Canes
19 holes x 18 holes
Cut 1

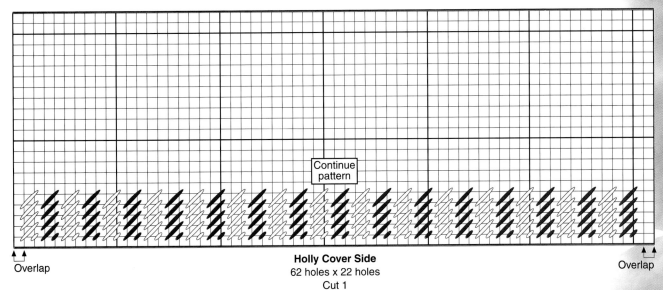

Continue
pattern

Overlap

Overlap

Holly Cover Side
62 holes x 22 holes
Cut 1

Christmas   Christmas   Christmas   Christmas   Christmas   Christmas

Even Santa has to do laundry! Hang this delightful garland across a mantel, doorway or shelf for lots of holiday cheer!

Skill Level: Beginner

Finished Size
Approximately 25" W x 7" H

Materials

- 1 sheet Darice Ultra Stiff 7-count plastic canvas
- Coats & Clark Red Heart Classic worsted weight yarn Art. E267 as listed in color key
- Darice Bright Jewels metallic cord as listed in color key
- Chenille acrylic yarn as listed in color key
- #16 tapestry needle
- ¼" white pompom
- 22" ⅛" metallic cording in color desired (sample used red, white and gold)
- 1" wooden spring clothes pins: 5 green and 3 red
- Hot-glue gun

Instructions

1. Cut plastic canvas according to graphs (pages 167 and 168).

2. Stitch pieces following graphs, reversing one mitten, one mitten cuff, one sleeve cuff, one pants cuff and one boot before stitching.

3. Overcast belt buckle with silver metallic cord. Overcast striped

Christmas Christmas Christmas Christmas Christmas Christmas

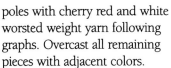

Pole Top
8 holes x 8 holes
Cut 2

Hat Cuff
9 holes x 12 holes
Cut 1

Attach cuff →

Hat
9 holes x 18 holes
Cut 1

Striped Pole
4 holes x 43 holes
Cut 2

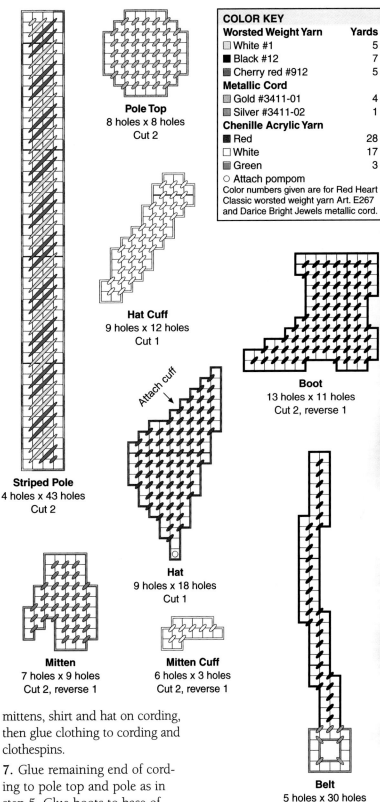

Boot
13 holes x 11 holes
Cut 2, reverse 1

Mitten
7 holes x 9 holes
Cut 2, reverse 1

Mitten Cuff
6 holes x 3 holes
Cut 2, reverse 1

Belt
5 holes x 30 holes
Cut 1

poles with cherry red and white worsted weight yarn following graphs. Overcast all remaining pieces with adjacent colors.

4. Using photo as a guide through step 7, glue cuffs to corresponding pieces. Glue pompom to tip of hat where indicated on graph. Glue shirt collar and shirt hem trim to shirt.

5. Glue one end of cording to back of one pole top, then glue pole top to top of one striped pole.

6. Evenly space belt, pants,

mittens, shirt and hat on cording, then glue clothing to cording and clothespins.

7. Glue remaining end of cording to pole top and pole as in step 5. Glue boots to base of one pole.

Christmas   Christmas   Christmas   Christmas   Christmas   Christmas

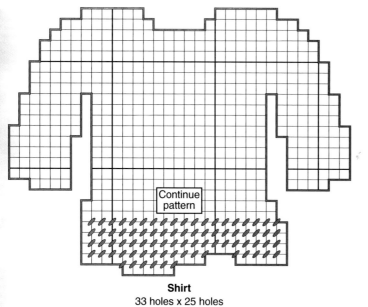

Shirt
33 holes x 25 holes
Cut 1

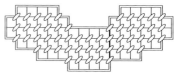

Shirt Collar
16 holes x 6 holes
Cut 1

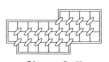

Sleeve Cuff
9 holes x 4 holes
Cut 2, reverse 1

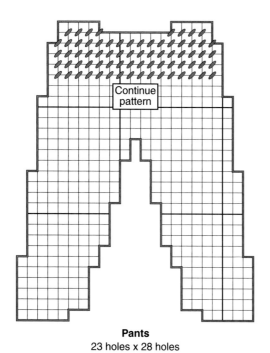

Pants
23 holes x 28 holes
Cut 1

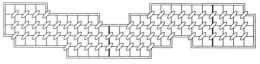

Shirt Hem Trim
24 holes x 5 holes
Cut 1

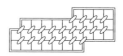

Pants Cuff
10 holes x 4 holes
Cut 2, reverse 1

Christmas   Christmas   Christmas   Christmas   Christmas   Christmas

CHICKADEE
Basket

Design by Janelle Giese

*Glued onto a small basket and accented with a straw bow,
this realistic-looking chickadee makes a charming winter accent!*

Skill Level: Beginner

Finished Size

Chickadee: 4" W x 4" H

Materials

- ⅓ sheet 7-count plastic canvas
- Uniek Needloft plastic canvas yarn as listed in color key
- DMC 6-strand embroidery floss as listed in color key
- #16 tapestry needle
- 7 Mill Hill Products ruby #05025 glass pebble beads from Gay Bowles Sales Inc.
- Raffia straw
- Small basket (sample basket is 5½" W x 4¼" H x 3½" D excluding handle)
- Thick white glue

Instructions

1. Cut plastic canvas according to graph.

2. Stitch and Overcast piece following graph.

3. Using 12 strands embroidery floss, work Cross Stitch for eye, then work Backstitches around completed Cross Stitch. Work French Knot in corner of eye with 6 strands white embroidery floss.

4. Backstitch wing with three strands black floss. Straight Stitch over wing with 3 strands white embroidery floss.

5. Work forest Lark's Head Knots, allowing loops of knots to face as shown on graphs.

6. Using 4 strands black embroidery floss, attach ruby pebble beads where indicated on graph. Trim Lark's Head Knots to ¾",

COLOR KEY

Plastic Canvas Yarn	Yards
■ Black #00	2
■ Cinnamon #14	1
■ Gray #38	2
□ Beige #40	1
□ White #41	1
□ Peach #47	1
⌒ Forest #29 Lark's Head Knot	1
6-Strand Embroidery Floss	
⁄ White Straight Stitch	1
⁄ Black #310 Backstitch	2
✕ Black #310 Cross Stitch	
○ White French Knot	
● Attach bead	

Color numbers given are for Uniek Needloft plastic canvas yarn and DMC 6-strand embroidery floss.

then unravel yarn. Place a dab of glue behind each knot to secure.

7. Using photo as a guide, make loops from raffia straw so bow extends beyond stitched motif. Wrap center with black floss, then center and tie to basket front.

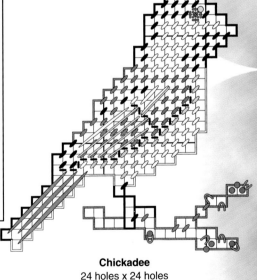

Chickadee
24 holes x 24 holes
Cut 1

8. Center chickadee over center of bow; attach to basket with floss, adding glue between motif, bow and basket for extra security.

CHICKADEE BASKET • 169

Christmas   Christmas   Christmas   Christmas   Christmas   Christmas

GINGERBREAD
Door Decor

Design by Jocelyn Sass

**Fabric strips worked over 5-count canvas make this charming
country door decoration a snap to stitch!**

Skill Level: Beginner

Finished Size

13¼" W x 17½" H excluding hanger

Materials

- 1 sheet 5-count plastic canvas
- 45"-wide fabric:
  - 1 yard sienna brown solid
  - ¼ yard off-white solid
  - ¼ yard coordinating print
- #16 tapestry needle
- 8 assorted buttons
- 1 yard 19-gauge wire
- Pencil
- Wire cutter
- Tacky glue

Project Notes

To thread needle, pull one corner of fabric strip through eye of needle.

Use short strips when working a small design area.

Fabric Preparation

1. Wash and dry all fabric.

2. Mark and clip edges every ½". Hold fabric firmly at each cut and pull to tear into strips. Discard first and last strips. Clip loose threads from strips.

Cutting and Stitching

1. Cut plastic canvas according to graph (page 172).

2. Stitch piece following graph, working off-white and print areas first, then working rows of sienna brown Slanting Gobelin Stitches. Overcast with sienna brown.

3. Using photo as a guide through step 6, glue four buttons to foot and four to arm.

4. Tear a 2" x 24" piece of print fabric and tie in a bow; trim ends. Glue bow to neckline.

5. Find center of 19-gauge wire. Using pencil, make two spirals on both sides of center.

6. Insert one end of wire from back to front in hole indicated on one shoulder. Twist to secure, then make a spiral in end. Repeat with other end of wire, inserting into other shoulder. 🎁

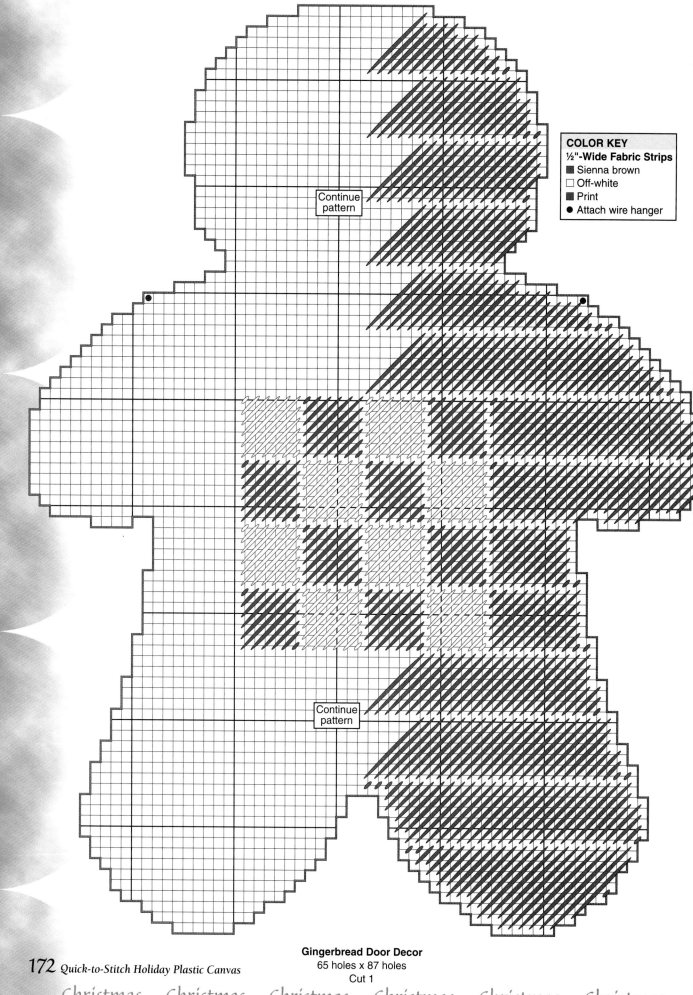

COLOR KEY
½"-Wide Fabric Strips
■ Sienna brown
□ Off-white
▦ Print
● Attach wire hanger

Continue
pattern

Continue
pattern

Gingerbread Door Decor
65 holes x 87 holes
Cut 1

Christmas   Christmas   Christmas   Christmas   Christmas   Christmas

We would like to acknowledge and thank the following designers whose original work has been published in this collection. We appreciate and value their creativity and dedication to designing quality plastic canvas projects!

Angie Arickx
Basket Bears Ornaments, Festive Banner & Coaster, Christmas Fridgie Frame, Golden Pendant, Hearts 'n' Stripes Mug & Coaster Set, Jack-o'-Lantern Hearts, Leprechaun Accents, Miniature Violet Basket, New Year's Bear, Patriotic Tissue Topper, Poinsettia Candy Dish, Pot o' Gold Favor, Santa Bear in the Chimney, Uncle Sam Teddy Bear, Star of David Magnet, Teddy Bear Valentine, Valentine Picture Hoop

Vicki Blizzard
Baby Bunny Basket, Cupcake Pokes, Dad's Dresser Box, Easter Pearls Ornaments, Gone Fishin' Door Hanger, Friendly Ghouls Lollipop Covers, Lazy Daisies Mug, Mama's Sleeping Door Hanger, Mother's Garden Photo Frames, Snowmen Centerpiece, Sow Lucky, Sunday Sails Mug, Sweet Hearts Pin, Touch of Gold Hanukkah Accents, Tulip Gift Bag, Whimsical Turkey Magnet

Ronda Bryce
Candy Corn Party Accents, Conversation Hearts Trio, Easter Sunday Bread Basket, Victorian Heart Potpourri Holder

Judy Collishaw
Haunted Gravestone Memo Holder, Toast the New Year Napkin Holder

Mary T. Cosgrove
Autumn Leaves Napkin Rings, Sweethearts Photo Frame

Kathleen J. Fischer
Shamrock Window Decoration, Star-Spangled Star

Janelle Giese
Chickadee Basket, Christmas Ornament Cuties, Easter Egg Animals, Little Pilgrims Basket, Pumpkin Greeting, Rocket Sam

Joan Green
Christmas Treat Spoon Toppers, Easter Egg Door Decoration, Halloween Wind Chimes, Mother's Triple Photo Frame, St. Nick Pillow Topper

Kathleen Hurley
Boughs of Holly Place Mat, Holiday Beverage Covers, Snowman Door Hanger

Carol Krob
Autumn Table Accessories

Celia Lange & Martha Bleidner of Celia Lange Designs
Garden Trellis Clock, Furry Friends Gift Stockings, Ghosts & Graves Basket, Hanukkah Bear Candy Dish, Pilgrim & Indian Wall Decor, Santa's Clothesline Garland, Times Square Party Hat

Alida Macor
Love Notes

Robin Petrina
Patriotic Welcome, Turkey Napkin Holder

Terry A. Ricioli
Harvesttime Wall Decor

Jocelyn Sass
Gingerbread Door Decor

Laura Scott
Log Cabin Coaster Set

Kimberly A. Suber
Halloween Door Hangers

Christine Westerberg
Spooky Accents

Linda Wyszynski
Shamrock Pin

STITCH Guide

Use the following diagrams to expand your plastic canvas stitching skills. For each diagram, bring needle up through canvas at the red number one and go back down through the canvas at the red number two. The second stitch is numbered in green. Always bring needle up through the canvas at odd numbers and take it back down through the canvas at the even numbers.

Background Stitches

The following stitches are used for filling in large areas of canvas. The Continental Stitch is the most commonly used stitch. Other stitches, such as the Condensed Mosaic and Scotch Stitch, fill in large areas of canvas more quickly than the Continental Stitch because their stitches cover a larger area of canvas.

Continental Stitch

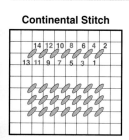

Condensed Mosaic

Running Stitch

Alternating Continental

Cross Stitch

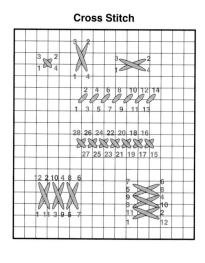

Long Stitch   **Slanting Gobelin**   **Scotch Stitch**

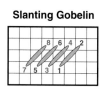

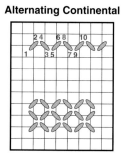

Embroidery Stitches

These stitches are worked on top of a stitched area to add detail to the project. Embroidery stitches are usually worked with one strand of yarn, several strands of pearl cotton or several strands of embroidery floss.

Lattice Stitch

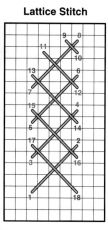

Chain Stitch

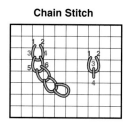

Straight Stitch

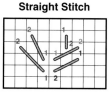

Fly Stitch

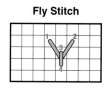

Couching

Backstitch

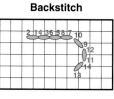

Stitch Guide   Stitch Guide   Stitch Guide   Stitch Guide   Stitch Guide

Embroidery Stitches

French Knot

Bring needle up through canvas.

Wrap yarn around needle 2 or 3 times, depending on desired size of knot; take needle back through canvase through same hole.

Lazy Daisy

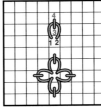

Bring yarn needle up through canvas, then back down in same hole, leaving a small loop.

Then, bring needle up inside loop; take needle back down through canvas on other side of loop.

Loop Stitch or Turkey Loop Stitch

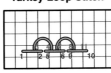

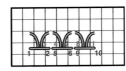

The top diagram shows this stitch left intact. This is an effective stitch for giving a project dimensional hair. The bottom diagram demonstrates the cut loop stitch. Because each stitch is anchored, cutting it will not cause the stitches to come out. A group of cut loop stitches gives a fluffy, soft look and feel to your project.

Specialty Stitches

The following stitches can be worked either on top of a previously stitched area or directly onto the canvas. Like the embroidery stitches, these too add wonderful detail and give your stitching additional interest and texture.

Diamond Eyelet

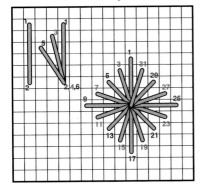

For each stitch, bring needle up at odd numbers around outside and take needle down through canvas at center hole.

Smyrna Cross

Satin Stitches

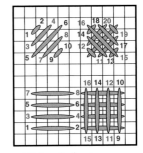

This stitch gives a "padded" look to your work.

Finishing Stitches

Overcast/Whipstitch

Overcasting and Whipstitching are used to finish the outer edges of the canvas. Overcasting is done to finish one edge at a time. Whipstitch is used to stitch two or more pieces of canvas together along on edge. For both Overcasting and Whipstitching, work one stitch in each hole along straight edges and inside corners, and two or three stitches in outside corners.

Lark's Head Knot

The Lark's Head Knot is used for a fringe edge or for attaching a hanging loop.

BUYER'S
Guide

When looking for a specific material, first check your local craft and retail stores. If you are unable to locate a product locally, contact the manufacturers listed below for the closest retail source in your area or a mail-order source.

Aleene's, a division of Duncan Enterprises
5673 E. Shields Ave.
Fresno, CA 93727
(800) 237-2642
www.duncan-enterprises.com

The Beadery
P.O. Box 178
Hope Valley, RI 02832
(401) 539-2432

Bucilla Corp.
1 Oak Ridge Rd.
Humboldt Industrial Park
Hazelton, PA 18201-9764
(800) 233-3239

Coats & Clark
Consumer Service
P.O. Box 12229
Greenville, SC 29612-0229
(800) 648-1479
www.coatsandclark.com

Daniel Enterprises
P.O. Box 1105
Laurinburg, NC 28353
(910) 277-7441

Darice Inc.
Mail-order source:
Bolek's
P.O. Box 465
330 N. Tuscarawas Ave.
Dover, OH 44622
(330) 364-8878

Delta Technical Coatings Inc.
2550 Pellissier Pl.
Whittier, CA 90601-1505
(800) 423-4135
www.deltacrafts.com

DMC Corp.
Hackensack Ave. Bldg. 10A
South Kearny, NJ 07032-4688
(800) 275-4117
www.dmc-usa.com

Elmore-Pisgah Inc.
P.O. Box 311
Rutherfordton, NC 28139
(800) 633-7829

Forster Inc./Diamond Brands
1800 Cloquet Ave.
Cloquet, MN 55720
(218) 879-6700

Gay Bowles Sales Inc.
P.O. Box 1060
Janesville, WI 53545
(800) 447-1332
www.millhill.com

Kreinik Mfg. Co. Inc.
3106 Timanus Ln., #101
Baltimore, MD 21244-2871
(800) 537-2166

Kunin Felt Co./Foss Mfg. Co. Inc.
P.O. Box 5000
Hampton, NH 03842-5000
(800) 292-7900
www.kuninfelt.com

Lion Brand Yarn Co.
34 W. 15th St.
New York, NY 10011
(800) 795-5466

Madeira Threads
9631 N.E. Colfax St.
Portland, OR 97220-1232
(800) 542-4727
www.madeirathreads.com/scs

Maxwell Wellington
1140 Monticello Rd.
P.O. Box 244
Madison, GA 30650
(800) 449-4996

National Artcraft Co.
7996 Darrow Rd.
Twinsburg, OH 44087
(888) 937-2723
www.nationalartcraft.com

**C.M. Offray & Son Inc./
Lion Ribbon Co. Inc.**
Rte. 24, Box 601
Chester, NJ 07930
(800) 551-LION
www.offray.com

Paper Adventures
P.O. Box 04393
Milwaukee, WI 53204-0393
(800) 727-0268
www.paperadventures.com

Rainbow Gallery
Mail-order source:
Designs by Joan Green
1130 Tollgate Dr.
Oxford, OH 45056
(513) 523-2690

Spinrite Inc.
P.O. Box 435
Lockport, NY 14094-0435
(800) 265-2864

Box 40
Listowel, Ontario N4W 3H3
Canada
(519) 291-3780

Sudberry House LLC.
12 Colton Rd.
East Lyme, CT 06333
(800) 243-2607
www.sudberry.com

Uniek
Mail-order source:
Annie's Attic Catalog
1 Annie Ln.
Big Sandy, TX 75755
(800) 582-6643

Walnut Hollow Farm Inc.
1409 State Rd. 23
Dodgeville, WI 53533-2112
(800) 950-5101

Westrim Crafts/Western Trimming Corp.
9667 Canoga Ave.
Chatsworth, CA 91311
(818) 998-8550

Yarn Tree Designs Inc.
P.O. Box 724
Ames, IA 50010
(800) 247-3952
www.yarntree.com

Buyer's Guide   Buyer's Guide   Buyer's Guide   Buyer's Guide   Buyer's Guide